Crisis in the Congo

Crisis in the Congo

A United Nations Force in Action

■

ERNEST W. LEFEVER

STUDIES OF U.S. POLICY AND THE U.N.

THE BROOKINGS INSTITUTION • WASHINGTON, D.C.

© 1965 by

THE BROOKINGS INSTITUTION

Published April 1965

Library of Congress Catalogue Card Number 65-19040

THE BROOKINGS INSTITUTION is an independent organization devoted to nonpartisan research, education, and publication in economics, government, foreign policy, and the social sciences generally. Its principal purposes are to aid in the development of sound public policies and to promote public understanding of issues of national importance.

The Institution was founded December 8, 1927, to merge the activities of the Institute for Government Research, founded in 1916, the Institute of Economics, founded in 1922, and the Robert Brookings Graduate School of Economics and Government, founded in 1924.

The general administration of the Institution is the responsibility of a self-perpetuating Board of Trustees. The Trustees are likewise charged with maintaining the independence of the staff and fostering the most favorable conditions for creative research and education. The immediate direction of the policies, program, and staff of the Institution is vested in the President, assisted by the division directors and an advisory council, chosen from the professional staff of the Institution.

In publishing a study, the Institution presents it as a competent treatment of a subject worthy of public consideration. The interpretations and conclusions in such publications are those of the author or authors and do not purport to represent the views of the other staff members, officers, or trustees of the Brookings Institution.

Foreword

THE CONGO has been a synonym for chaos and confusion ever since Belgian authority was abruptly withdrawn in the summer of 1960. Strategically located in the heart of Africa, nearly the size of Western Europe, and rich in resources, the new republic became the object of international attention within a week after independence day. When the Leopoldville government was unable to cope with the mutiny of its soldiers and the ensuing panic, it requested military assistance from the United Nations. The resulting four-year peacekeeping effort between 1960 and 1964 was the largest, most complex, and most costly operation ever carried out by the United Nations.

In this study of the Congo experience, special attention is given to the role of the United States without whose diplomatic, financial, and logistical support the operation could neither have been mounted nor sustained. The author, Ernest W. Lefever, examines the political, military, legal, and financial aspects of the novel effort and concludes with a general appraisal of the operation and observations which bear on the future prospects for internationally authorized peacekeeping missions.

Relying almost exclusively on primary sources, including interviews with many of the principal actors in the Congo drama, the author analyzes the peacekeeping experience within the larger crucible of international politics. The operation is seen as a reflection of the widespread interest in decolonization and the less widely shared interest in political stability in Central

Africa. As such it provides a background for what promises to be a continuing crisis in the Congo as well as for political developments south of the Sahara generally.

Crisis in the Congo is part of a new program of United Nations policy studies financed by the Ford Foundation. The program, which is supervised by Arthur M. Cox, as part of the Foreign Policy Studies Division directed by H. Field Haviland, Jr., has as its principal purpose the independent analysis of critical issues of U.S. policy concerning the United Nations and the specialized agencies. These studies dealing with political, economic, and social problems propose guidelines for policy to the U.S. government and provide background for more informed public discussion. The program also seeks to stimulate related work at other institutions throughout the country. In addition to Mr. Lefever's book dealing with U.N. peacekeeping in the Congo, a study is in progress dealing with U.N. civilian activities in the Congo, including efforts toward political conciliation.

Ernest W. Lefever is now a member of the Senior Staff of the Foreign Policy Studies Division at the Brookings Institution; but he wrote the present book for Brookings while on a one-year leave of absence from the Institute for Defense Analyses. Before that, Mr. Lefever had served as the Institute's study leader of a two-year research project for the Department of Defense on the role of international military forces. He was the principal author of its published report, *National Armaments and International Force* (1963). Mr. Lefever is still serving as Consultant to the Institute and also as an Adjunct Professor of International Relations at the American University. He has previously been associated with the Washington Center of Foreign Policy Research of the Johns Hopkins University and was Chief of the Foreign Affairs Division of the Library of Congress. Publications that he has written or edited include *Ethics and United States Foreign Policy* (1957), *The World Crisis and American Responsibility* (1958), *Profile of American Politics* (co-author, 1960), and *Arms and Arms Control* (1962).

The author and the Brookings Institution are grateful for

the helpful comments on the present book from an Advisory Committee consisting of Major General John B. Cary (USAF Ret.) of the Institute for Defense Analyses, Andrew W. Cordier of Columbia University, Lawrence S. Finkelstein of the Carnegie Endowment for International Peace, Francis O. Wilcox of the Johns Hopkins University, Colonel William O. Gall (USA) of the Department of Defense, and Alan W. Ford, J. Wayne Fredericks, Jonathan Dean, Elmore Jackson, James L. O'Sullivan, and Nathan Pelcovits, all of the Department of State. Mr. Pelcovits and Mr. Finkelstein also served on the Reading Committee.

The author wishes to express his gratitude to more than a hundred key participants or observers in the Congo drama from fifteen countries who provided valuable information and insight for the study. Though for reasons of propriety most of these persons cannot be identified by name, eight men who have served in the Congo deserve special mention here: Ambassadors Clare H. M. Timberlake and Edmund A. Gullion; Lewis Hoffacker, and Jonathan Dean, both former Consuls in Elisabethville; Colonel Knut Raudstein, U.S. Army Attache in Leopoldville; Lieutenant General Kebede Gebre, U.N. Force Commander; Major General D. Prem Chand, U.N. Commander in Katanga; and Brigadier General Reginald Noronha, a U.N. commander in Elisabethville. The author is also indebted to members of the United Nations Secretariat. At the U.S. Mission to the United Nations he was generously assisted throughout the study by Colonel Clarence Nelson (USA), and Colonel Arthur B. Swan (USAF).

At Brookings, in addition to Mr. Haviland and Mr. Cox, the author wishes to express his appreciation to several persons who are now his colleagues. These include Robert E. Asher and Ruth B. Russell, who served on the Reading Committee. To Miss Russell, whose *United Nations Experience with Military Forces: Political and Legal Aspects* is closely related to the present study, he owes a special debt for her editorial and substantive counsel throughout the project. He wishes to express his appreciation to Wynfred Joshua who helped put the finishing touches on the manuscript and to Barbara P. Haskins for her thoughtful editing.

Brookings is grateful to the Institute for Defense Analyses for encouraging the project and for making available the services of Mr. Lefever while he was still on the Institute's staff.

The interpretations and conclusions of the author do not necessarily represent the views of the persons consulted, nor of the trustees, the officers, or other staff members of the Brookings Institution.

ROBERT D. CALKINS
President

February 1965
The Brookings Institution
1775 Massachusetts Avenue, N.W.
Washington, D.C.

Contents

Crisis in the Congo

1

The Rise and Fall of Lumumba

The First Ninety Days

We are going to show the world what the black man can do when he works in freedom, and we are going to make the Congo the center of radiance for the whole of Africa. PATRICE LUMUMBA, JUNE 30, 1960

INDEPENDENCE DAY IN LEOPOLDVILLE was outwardly calm. On that June day in 1960, everything went according to schedule, with one important exception. Congolese troops, still under the command of Belgian officers, were controlling all ceremonial areas. The population was in a subdued holiday mood, seemingly unaware that history was being made.

King Baudouin had flown in from Brussels to take part in the transfer of authority from Belgium to the new Congolese leaders.

President Eisenhower had sent a bust of Abraham Lincoln to the new Government, and the United States announced that it would provide scholarships for 300 Congolese students to study abroad.

Dr. Ralph J. Bunche, United Nations Undersecretary for Special Political Affairs, was present to represent the world organization and to work out plans for technical assistance to the new state.

At the morning independence ceremonies King Baudouin delivered a friendly speech before the assembled dignitaries of the world. Joseph Kasavubu, the first President of the

3

Congo, responded in kind. Both men spoke of an expected era of mutual cooperation between Brussels and Leopoldville, symbolized by the Treaty of Friendship signed the day before.

Then the surface calm was suddenly shattered by the speech of a tall man wearing a goatee and the mauve-red sash of Belgium's top decoration, the Order of Leopold. The man was Patrice Lumumba, a former postal clerk who had become the Congo's most persuasive nationalist leader and its first Prime Minister. Though he called Belgium a "friendly country," he promptly denounced the colonial legacy as one of "atrocious sufferings" and "humiliating bondage," filled with "ironies, insults, blows which we had to endure morning, noon, and night because we were 'Negroes.'"

Against this dark backdrop of brutal "colonial oppression," Lumumba painted a bright new Congo of "peace, prosperity, and grandeur," to be built by the Congo's "own children." He declared that the "peace of guns and bayonets" would be replaced by a "peace of courage and good will."[1]

Western observers as well as President Kasavubu and other moderate Congolese were shocked by the speech which they regarded as strident, contemptuous, and ill-tempered.

During an exchange of toasts a few hours later, Lumumba spoke in a different mood. He thanked King Baudouin and "the noble Belgian people" for their decision to grant independence, and expressed the hope that the collaboration between the two governments would be "long and durable."

Lumumba was a complicated man. He was the child of Africa and of the West and had an ambivalent attitude toward both parents. He was highly critical of Congolese "tribal quarrels which exhaust our strength and make us contemptible to the foreigner." He both appreciated and despised Belgium. His outlook was further confused by the fact that he had been wooed and cultivated by the Communist bloc during the

[1] The text of Lumumba's address, June 30, 1960, is carried in Alan P. Merriam, *Congo: Background of Conflict* (Northwestern University Press, 1961), pp. 352-54.

two years before independence. He was assailed by conflict-ing pressures and demands from these three worlds and, as such, he personified the restless Congo itself. Lumumba on independence day was a living symbol of the tragedy and torment that were about to overtake the new republic.

The Republic of the Congo became a state before it became a nation. With a diverse population of 13.8 million people belonging to more than 200 different tribes, there was virtually no sense of national identity. The great majority of urban workers were only partially detribalized, and most of them did not think of themselves as Congolese. The concept of a loyalty and patriotism which transcended the tribe and embraced the whole nation could be found among a small number of Westernized Congolese, and then usually only in a rudimentary form. The fundamental problem of the Congo was, and still is, to build a sense of common identity and loyalty among its many peoples strong enough to sustain a genuine national government.

When Belgian colonial authority, the only source of cohesion and coherence in the vast central African country, was abruptly withdrawn, the endemic centrifugal forces of tribalism, geographical diversity, and political rivalry were unleashed. Within four days the Congo erupted in open violence and conflict. At this point President Kasavubu and Prime Minister Lumumba knew they desperately needed outside military assistance and they had to make up their minds where to turn for help. Should they seek aid from governments committed to peaceful and gradual political development, or from governments committeed to violent and revolutionary methods?

The Congo crisis, though similar to crises in other newly independent states, was more urgent than most and in important respects unique. The very size and strategic location of the country made it impossible for the problem to go unheeded in the chancelleries of the world.

The Congo is to Africa what India is to South Asia, and

what Brazil is to South America. Almost the size of Western Europe, the Congo shares frontiers with nine states and stretches from the Atlantic to Lake Tanganyika. By tropical African standards, the Congo has advanced industrial, plantation, and transportation systems, thanks to substantial capital investment from Europe during the colonial period. The total annual production in 1959, for example, was $1.2 billion, 40 percent of which was exported. The per capita income was $88, yet this supported one of the highest living standards in "Black Africa."[2] The entire economy of the country continues to be dominated by a few large Belgian holding companies in which the Belgian government is a major shareholder. With its actual and potential wealth, the Congo is a country whose political and economic future is of more than passing interest to the United States, the Soviet Union, and many other states.

The Belgian Colonial Legacy

The Belgian interest in developing the Congo economically was not matched by an interest in developing its people politically. This almost exclusively material interest was expressed by King Baudouin in February 1960, when he addressed the Congolese political leaders at the conclusion of the Brussels Round Table Conference at which independence was promised. Describing the colonial legacy, he said, "The Belgians were able to establish safety, peace, and all the other prerequisites of prosperity in the heart of Central Africa."

In contrast to many other new African states, the Congo had virtually no effective preparation for the responsibilities of self-government. The paternalistic Belgian administration did not seriously acknowledge the Congolese right to independence until after the first outbreak of political rioting which occurred in Leopoldville in January 1959. Hence, Brussels did not provide an adequate program of prepara-

[2] Edward Marcus, "An Economic Appraisal of the Belgian Congo," *The Belgian Congo Today*, Vol. 9 (April-May 1960), p. 22.

tion immediately before independence; nor did Brussels provide the longer period of political apprenticeship which was tried with varying degrees of effectiveness in the British and French African territories.[3]

The Belgian failure to prepare the Congolese for political responsibility and the belated recognition of the political forces at work in Africa were rooted in the paternalistic and materialistic interpretation of Belgian responsibility. When A. A. J. van Bilsen of the Institute for Colonial Studies in Antwerp proposed in 1955 a thirty-year plan leading to independence, he was widely regarded in Belgium as a radical. It took the shock of President de Gaulle's speech in Brazzaville on August 24, 1958, offering French colonies immediate independence or membership in the French Community, to awaken Brussels to the dimly perceived political stirrings within its own Congo. But it was already too late to make up for lost time. The fact that "a progressive evolution was too long delayed, and that the Congo had not been sufficiently prepared for its own responsibilities" was soon to be recognized by many Belgian political leaders and scholars including W. J. Ganshof van der Meersch, the Belgian Minister of African Affairs who had served as Resident Minister in the Congo during the months in 1960 preceding independence.[4]

The Belgian Congo was administered by the Colonial Ministry in Brussels through a Governor-General and a Governor for each of the six provinces: Leopoldville, Equateur, Orientale, Kasai, Kivu, and Katanga. Political parties emerged for the first time in 1957 with the holding of the first elections in the Congo. These elections were restricted to a ballot for local officials in the three largest cities: Leopoldville, Elisabethville, and Jadotville.

It was only after the Leopoldville riots in early 1959 and the

[3] Alan P. Merriam, *Congo: Background of Conflict* (Northwestern University Press, 1961), pp. 29-65. See also Fernand Van Langenhove, *The Congo and the Problems of Decolonisation* (Brussels: Institut Royal des Relations Internationales, 1960), pp. 1-10 and 19-26.

[4] W. J. Ganshof van der Meersch, *Fin de la Souveraineté Belge au Congo* (Brussels: Institut Royal des Relations Internationales, 1963), p. 596.

first public acknowledgement of the right to independence that Brussels advanced a plan for extending the franchise up to the provincial level. On October 16, 1959, the Belgians announced that a Congolese central government would be established the following year. The dissatisfaction of Congolese political leaders, who regarded these measures as too cautious, led to the convening of the Brussels Round Table Conference in January 1960. A four-year plan for a transitional period to independence was presented at the conference by Belgian administrators in the Congo, but in the prevailing atmosphere of tension and anxiety, the Congolese supported Lumumba's strident demand for immediate independence. Eager to avoid a "Belgian Algeria" and confident that European economic interests in the Congo would not be seriously jeopardized, the Belgian government announced that it would grant sovereignty to the Congo on June 30, less than five months away. This decision was regarded by close observers as an act of panic, if not of irresponsibility.

Independence day found the Congolese unprepared for the burdens of self-government. There were no broad parties with national appeal. The tribally based parties were run by untrained men. The eleventh-hour extension of the franchise at the local level gave the people no real experience in self-government. Further, with very rare exceptions, the Congolese had no experience in civil administration, except at the lowest levels. Some 9,000 top and middle-range administrative positions were still held by Belgians on July 1, 1960. It was assumed that these civil servants, most of whom had planned to remain, would continue to hold their positions in the new government until Congolese could eventually be trained to replace them. Since it was only in 1957 that the Belgians had started to take a small number of Congolese into the middle range of the civil administration, the process of Africanization was expected to take many years. The same general pattern of European domination also prevailed in the economic sector.

The Belgian educational policy did not provide the training

essential to political leadership and administrative responsibility in spite of the fact that the Congo had one of the highest literacy rates in Africa, estimated at 40 to 60 percent.[5] The educational pyramid had a broad base, but it came to a blunt peak at the secondary level. In 1958, some 1,400,000 children were receiving primary education, mainly in government-subsidized Roman Catholic schools. There was, however, little education above the age of fourteen. Fewer than 25,000 Congolese had received any secondary education at all, and at independence there were only about thirty Congolese university graduates in the entire country. A small number of students had advanced beyond the secondary level, mainly in preparation for the priesthood in Catholic mission schools. Congolese were not encouraged to pursue higher education abroad, and there was no university in the Congo until 1954 when Lovanium opened its doors in Leopoldville. At independence, only thirteen Africans had been graduated from Lovanium.[6] A university was also opened in Elisabethville in 1956.

The Belgian policy of not training Congolese for responsible positions was also followed in the *Force publique*, which in 1960 was a 25,000-man national security force combining the functions of an army and a police establishment. The *Force* was entirely officered by 1,100 Europeans, mainly Belgians. Few educational facilities were available to the largely illiterate Congolese troops, though a small number were selected to learn trades needed in the *Force*. Its mission was to maintain law and order, protect property, and secure the border.

Discipline within the *Force publique* under the Belgians was, by African army standards, excellent. Life on and off duty was carefully regulated. The Congolese soldier accepted the harsh discipline well and felt that his new way of life was superior to tribal ways. He was loyal to the *Force publique* as an institution and a way of life, but not to the state or nation, which to him was merely

[5] Helen Kitchen (ed.), *The Educated African* (Praeger, 1962), pp. 192-93.
[6] Colin Legum (ed.), *Africa: A Handbook to the Continent* (Praeger, 1962), p. 195. Some sources maintain no Congolese had actually graduated from Lovanium University by June 30, 1960.

a foreign power represented by Belgian officers. He readily fired upon his own countrymen provided they did not belong to his own tribe. As a result, troops employed in punitive operations against Congolese were regularly drawn from distant parts of the country. The civilian [African] population regarded the *Force publique* with respect born of fear.[7]

Subsequent events were soon to confirm the validity of this portrait of the Congolese soldier as loyal neither to state nor nation. On June 30, 1960, the *Force publique* became the Congolese National Army (*Armée Nationale Congolaise—* ANC). This was largely an exercise in nomenclature because no significant changes in the functions or command structure of the *Force* were planned or anticipated. Like the Belgian civil administrators, until the very eve of independence most of the *Force* officers assumed that independence would bring little change; they planned to continue in their posts until Congolese could be trained and commissioned to replace them, and there was little sense of urgency about such training. The prevailing attitude was expressed by Lieutenant General Emil Janssens, the *Force* commander, who assumed that the white officers would continue to serve the new republic as they had the Belgian Congo. He expressed his view graphically on the blackboard of the officers mess in Camp Leopold II: "Before Independence = After Independence."[8] This celebrated statement soon became a symbol of Belgium's illusory expectations in the new Congo.

The First Fourteen Days

The inauspicious birth of the Republic of the Congo was a prologue to disaster. The rapidly exploding events of the first

[7] U.S. Army, *Area Handbook for the Republic of the Congo (Leopoldville)*, Special Operations Research Office, American University (U.S. Government Printing Office, 1962), pp. 622-23.

[8] Centre de Recherche et d'Information Socio-Politiques, *Congo: 1960*, Vol. I prepared by J. Gérard-Libois and Benoit Verhaegen (Brussels: Les Dossiers du CRISP, n.d.), p. 372. (Hereinafter cited as CRISP, *Congo: 1960*, or *Congo: 1961*, etc.)

two weeks set the stage for a tragicomic drama that was played before the eyes of the world in the four ensuing years. On the third day of independence—on July 2, 1960—tribal disorders erupted in Leopoldville and Luluabourg. Three days later, on July 5, Congolese soldiers in Thysville and Leopoldville mutinied against their Belgian officers, mainly because they wanted some of the material and psychological rewards of their civilian counterparts in the Central Government. The mutiny was probably encouraged by Communist bloc agents who had infiltrated the country. In the spreading disorder, property was destroyed and some Europeans were killed or injured. Many of the 100,000 Belgian citizens living in the Congo were terror-stricken. During the night of July 7–8 alone, more than 1,300 women and children, mostly Belgians, fled in panic across the Congo River to Brazzaville.

After the mutiny, Belgian authorities tried to persuade Lumumba and other Congolese officials to permit Belgian metropolitan troops then stationed in the Congo to restore order. These troops (not associated with the former *Force publique*) were confined to the two large Belgian bases, one at Kitona on the Atlantic coast, and the other at Kamina in the province of Katanga. Both bases were held by Brussels under the Treaty of Friendship signed on the eve of independence, but not approved by the new Congolese Parliament. Lumumba refused to let Belgium use its troops. Some observers believe that if it had not been for Lumumba's intransigence, the other Congo leaders would have requested, or at least permitted, the Belgians to restore order.

After five days of fruitless efforts, Belgian patience wore thin, and on July 9, against the wishes of the Congo government, Brussels flew in an additional two and one-half companies of paratroopers from Belgium to reinforce the two bases. This reinforcement in itself was probably not a violation of the treaty, but the subsequent deployment of Belgian troops outside the bases to restore order and protect Belgian lives, without the permission of Leopoldville, clearly was. The Belgian soldiers did not leave their bases until July 10, eight days after the original rioting, and only after the mutinies had spread to Katanga. They intervened in Elisabethville, Jadotville, Kamina, and elsewhere, and restored order. By July 19, Belgian forces in the Congo totalled 10,000 men.

When the mutinous Congolese soldiers closed the ferry to Brazzaville, the United States provided transport planes and helicopters to supplement Sabena aircraft in evacuating frightened whites. Before long, a substantial portion of the European population had fled. This exodus robbed the Congo of the experienced people who had planned to remain as advisers and technical experts and without whom the Congolese could not manage their political, military, or economic affairs.

Within days the ANC ceased to exist as a cohesive and disciplined army. Lieutenant General Janssens and the great majority of European officers were summarily dismissed and replaced by inexperienced Congolese noncommissioned officers. On July 9, President Kasavubu, in his function as Commander in Chief of the Army, and Prime Minister Lumumba, acting as Minister of National Defense, promoted former Sergeant Major Victor Lundula to Major General and put him in command of the ANC with Joseph Mobutu as his Chief of Staff.

To further complicate matters, on July 11, President Moise Tshombe of Katanga proclaimed his province an independent state. This action was taken, he said, to secede from chaos and because Lumumba was following a Communist line. He appealed for Belgian military aid to uphold his regime, at the same time criticizing the United States for not supporting him.

Katangan secession was only in part an expression of indigenous "nationalist" sentiment. The political leaders of northern Katanga, which is Baluba territory, were actively opposed to secession. The population of Katanga was never consulted on the matter.[9] From the beginning, secession was a political

---

[9] In February 1960, Tshombe's Conakat party won only 25 out of a total of 60 seats in the Katanga Parliament. The major opposition group, the Balubakat Cartel in North Katanga, won 23 seats. The Balubakat and their allies, both of which subsequently opposed secession, polled 134,916 votes against 91,116 for the Conakat party and its allies.

stratagem designed to preserve the comparative wealth of Katanga and to advance the interests of Tsombe and his political supporters, the Belgian residents in the province, and the foreign investors in Union Minière du Haut-Katanga and other economic enterprises in Katanga. With only 10 percent of the Congo's population, Katanga in 1960 provided about 50 percent of the Congo's revenue. It produced about 8 percent of the world's copper, 60 percent of its cobalt, and important quantities of radium, uranium, zinc, and other minerals. In 1959, Union Minière alone paid the Belgian government some $60 million in taxes. Ninety percent of the tax revenue from enterprises in the Congo was used to finance the colonial administration there.

On the same day, July 11, that Tshombe declared Katanga independent, Lumumba, on the advice of American Ambassador-designate Clare H. Timberlake, made an oral request for United Nations assistance to restore discipline in the ANC. This appeal was addressed to Ralph Bunche, who was representing the Secretary-General in Leopoldville at that time both at the independence ceremonies and in discussions on the establishment of a U.N. technical assistance program for the new state. Bunche immediately cabled the appeal to New York. Secretary-General Hammarskjold promptly convened the U.N. delegates from Ethiopia, Ghana, Guinea, Liberia, Libya, Morocco, Sudan, Tunisia, and the United Arab Republic to discuss possible African contributions to a program of "technical assistance in the security field" for the Congo. On the following day, July 12, before anything could be done about the original request, a formal written cable signed by Kasavubu and Lumumba reached the Secretary-General. It solicited urgent U.N. "military assistance" because of Belgian "aggression" and Belgian support of Katangan secession. Between the oral and written messages to the United Nations, the Congo Cabinet requested direct American assistance during Lumumba's absence. But President Dwight D. Eisenhower did as his ambassador had done the day before; he advised Leopoldville to seek help through the United Nations.

Lumumba's original oral overture to Bunche emphasized the

unreliability of the Congolese army and the inability of Leopoldville to maintain order, while the later written request to Hammarskjold focused on the "external aggression" and "colonialist machinations" of Belgium, which were described as "a threat to international peace" and a violation of the Brussels-Leopoldville Treaty of Friendship signed on the eve of independence.[10] The significant difference in tone between the two appeals was prompted largely by Belgian intervention to restore order. This difference reflected two fundamental ways of looking at the Congo problem. One emphasized the Congo's internal weakness and the other external interference. These basically diverging viewpoints influenced the U.N. debate on the Congo and the resulting resolutions. They were responsible for much of the tension between the Secretary-General and his supporters on the one hand, and Lumumba and his allies on the other. There were also differences of opinion among governments supporting Hammarskjold on the extent to which Belgian post-independence activities were responsible for the crisis.

When Lumumba learned that his Cabinet had formalized the earlier request for U.S. aid at the July 12 meeting during his absence, he was greatly disturbed, and sought the advice of the Soviet representatives in Leopoldville. On July 14, he persuaded Kasavubu to join him in a cable to Soviet Premier Nikita S. Khrushchev stating that the Congo "is occupied by Belgian troops and the lives of the Republic's President and Premier are in danger," and begging the Soviet Union "to watch hourly over the situation."[11] Khrushchev replied that Moscow would provide "any assistance that might be necessary for the victory" of the Congo's "just cause." This was the first of a number of friendly exchanges between Lumumba and the Soviet government. Eventually, the Russians provided some unilateral military aid.

Most of the perplexing problems which the United Nations and interested governments were to face in the four following

[10] See Appendix D for the text of the treaty.
[11] Ganshof van der Meersch, *op. cit.*, p. 477.

years were to be found, at least in embryo form, in those first fourteen hectic days. No one could predict the depth of the U.N. involvement initiated by the July 14 Security Council resolution which authorized the Secretary-General to make arrangements for military assistance to the Congo. Much less could anyone foresee that the quick response of the United Nations to the Congo's desperate plea would turn out to be the beginning of one of the most controversial international developments in recent decades. The peacekeeping force sent to the Congo has been by far the largest and most complex operation ever administered by an international organization.[12]

For nearly three years the United Nations Force (UNF) exceeded 15,000 men. At its height it included almost 20,000 men, officers, and specialized personnel from 35 states, compared with 6,465 men (including 1,711 British troops) in the Cyprus action as of June 1964. Because of the rotation of units, more than 93,000 men served in the UNF.[13] During its four years, the Congo operation was the overwhelming preoccupation of the Secretariat and a heavy strain on the administrative structure and financial resources of the Organization. The total cost of the military operation from July 1960 through June 1964, was $402 million, of which the United States provided slightly less than 42 percent, or $168.2 million. The U.S. contribution comprised both assessments and voluntary contributions. (The expenses for U.N. civilian operations in the Congo are not included in these figures.)

The Congo mission established new procedural and legal precedents, and precipitated a constitutional crisis at the United Nations, culminating in the unsuccessful Soviet demand for a Secretariat subject to a Communist veto. The Congo

[12] The forces under the unified U.N. command in Korea were much larger than those of the Congo undertaking, but the Korean effort was under the executive control of the United States. It was not financed through the United Nations. The Secretariat had no part in the operation or deployment of the force. The operation was carried on under the aegis of the United Nations, but only in the broadest sense did the Organization determine the terms of reference.

[13] U.N. Security Council, Nineteenth Year, *Official Records,* Doc. S/5784 (June 29, 1964), p. 38.

effort produced a major financial crisis for the Organization. The area also became a major arena of the struggle between the Communist bloc and the West, and the crucible in which the goals of decolonization and self-determination were severely and dramatically tested. It has been the primary foreign policy problem for Belgium and half a dozen African states; it has also been a major foreign policy question for many other governments including the United States, the Soviet Union, Britain, France, India, and Sweden.

Why Did the United Nations Intervene?

Since the end of World War II there have been scores of political crises and conflicts which have threatened the peace, at least in their local areas. According to two studies, there have been thirty-eight wars between 1945 and 1962, with an average duration of 5.8 years.[14] In the majority of cases when states in trouble could not deal with the situation themselves, they turned to a friend or ally for assistance. In January 1964, for example, the governments of Kenya, Tanganyika and Uganda requested direct military assistance from Britain, the former colonial power, to put down mutinous army units shortly after independence.

Since its beginning, the United Nations has authorized peacekeeping missions involving military personnel on eleven or twelve occasions, but never, with the exception of Korea, for other than observation or police functions. Among the many conflicts for which the Security Council was *not* requested to send a U.N. military presence were the Algerian war (1954-1962), the Mau Mau uprising in Kenya (1953-1955), the conflict in Cyprus (1955-1958), China-Burma

[14] These statistics have been derived from Evan Luard, *Peace and Opinion* (London: Oxford University Press, 1962), and L. F. Richardson, *Statistics of Deadly Quarrels* (Boxwood Press, 1960). See also Fielding Lewis Greaves, "'Peace' in Our Time," *The Military Review*, Vol. 42 (December 1962), pp. 55-58.

clashes (1950-1953), Cuba (1957-1959), and French Indo-China (1947-1954). The Council was not asked to act in these instances for a variety of reasons but chiefly because its permanent members could not agree on what action should be taken, even though each conflict was obviously a threat to or breach of the peace.

With this record of rare and limited involvement, why did the United Nations intervene so promptly in the Congo crisis? The simple and correct answer is that the Council had received a specific request for military assistance from a legitimate government, that the request was strongly endorsed by the United States, which did not want to become directly involved, and that it was not actively opposed by any other permanent member of the Council.

The Charter provides two ways by which the Security Council may authorize the dispatch of military personnel to a trouble spot. Under Article 42 (Chapter VII), the Council is authorized to *order* military operations "by air, sea, or land forces as may be necessary to maintain or restore international peace and security."[15] This mandatory authority to use sanctions has never been exercised by the Council, which even in the case of Korea only *recommended* that member states provide assistance to the Republic of Korea.

Under Chapter VI, the Council may "at any stage of a dispute" that is "likely to endanger the maintenance of international peace" *recommend* "appropriate procedures" or operations in the interests of pacific settlement. Under this general authority, and, at least by implication, under Articles 40 and 49 of Chapter VII, the Council authorized the Congo peacekeeping force. (The force could also be regarded as a "subsidiary organ" of the Security Council under Article 29.) A U.N. presence dispatched under this broad authority may be either military or civilian, and may range in size from one man to a force of 20,000 or more troops. A pacific settlement presence of this kind must have the consent of the host state

---

[15] See Appendix A for relevant articles of the U.N. Charter.

and other states directly involved and, by definition, is not a sanctions force, i.e., it may not take military action against any state.

Returning to the reasons for U.N. intervention in the Congo, perhaps the most important one was the fact that both the United States and the Soviet Union agreed initially that a peacekeeping force should be sent. This early accord between the two super powers was endorsed by six additional affirmative votes for the July 14 resolution. Neither France, which opposed the creation of a force, nor Britain, which had serious reservations about it, felt strongly enough to veto the resolution. The support of Argentina, Ecuador, and Italy reflected the general sentiment in the West. Neutralist support was indicated by the affirmative votes of Tunisia and Ceylon. Following the Soviet lead, Poland also supported the resolution.

This broad consensus was not based upon a common understanding of the crisis or of what the United Nations should do, but rather upon a minimal agreement that the Secretary-General should be authorized to do something. As seen by the supporting governments, there were two threats in the Congo crisis: the threat to international peace and the threat to successful decolonization. The dangers were weighted differently. Russia emphasized that the continued presence of Belgian troops was a threat to decolonization. Many of the neutralist states also focused upon Belgium as the chief danger. The United States emphasized both the threat to peace and to decolonization, but regarded the Soviet Union (acting directly or through cooperative states like Ghana, Guinea, or Egypt) rather than Belgium, as the chief problem. Washington also recognized the dangers of internal weakness, and was particularly concerned about the disruptive role of ANC units. Though there was some sentiment in the State Department for not getting involved at all in the Congo's security problem, the prevailing view was that the danger of Communist penetration was sufficiently great to support the use of a U.N. peacekeeping force.

Two and a half years after the event, Harlan Cleveland recalled the choices confronting the United States: "Should the Congo's chaos be attacked by a hastily assembled international peace force; or should we send in a division of United States Marines; or should we just sit on our hands and wait for our adversaries to exploit the situation?" We wisely decided, he said, "not to risk a confrontation of nuclear powers in the center of Africa." We believed that a U.N. force would serve "the national interest" of the United States and the great majority of U.N. members.[16]

Adlai Stevenson's statement that "the only way to keep the cold war out of the Congo is to keep the U.N. in the Congo,"[17] was more rhetorical than accurate. U.N. intervention both reflected and assured big-power interest in the local conflict. No crisis debated by the Security Council or the General Assembly is insulated from Cold War politics. The United States was not seeking to back out of a political contest with the Communist bloc in the Congo, but it wanted the contest to be conducted by acceptable rules and with minimum risk. This excluded unilateral military intervention by either side. The United States, with its anticolonial tradition and its increasing interest in the nonaligned world, did not want to offend the leaders of the new African and other neutralist states. It assumed that U.N. intervention, as opposed to U.S. bilateral assistance, would blunt the charges of neocolonialism. It was not clear at the time how much and what kind of assistance was required, but it was generally assumed that troops would have to become involved in police operations. The United States also had a general policy of playing a quiet

[16] Speech by Harlan Cleveland, Assistant Secretary of State for International Organization Affairs, Jan. 17, 1963 (U.S. Department of State Press Release 34), p. 3. A similar view had also been expressed by Undersecretary of State George W. Ball on Dec. 19, 1961, the text of which is reproduced in *The Elements in Our Congo Policy* (U.S. Department of State Publication 7326, December 1961), pp. 6-7.

[17] U.N. Security Council, Fifteenth Year, *Official Records*, 943rd Meeting (Feb. 15, 1961), p. 9.

supporting role to the former metropoles in dealings with the newly independent African states. Further, by the time Washington received a formal request from Leopoldville for assistance, the matter had already been brought to the attention of the Secretary-General.

The motives of states supporting the U.N. Force were mixed, reflecting their varying national interests and foreign policies. The affirmative action of the Council was a product of these conflicting motives. There was also the urgency of the problem, Dag Hammarskjold's initiative, and the fact that neither the Secretary-General nor any government could anticipate the political or financial cost of the novel enterprise or the international controversy it would precipitate.

Ironically, the Belgians who were militarily capable of restoring order were denied this constructive role, either bilaterally or under the aegis of the United Nations, primarily because of two facts. One was their deployment of paratroopers on July 10 which frightened and angered some Congolese leaders and led to charges of "aggression." The other fact was the anti-Belgian attitude of Lumumba who had been subjected to increasing Soviet influences and pressures. Though there were some joint U.N.–Belgian patrols in the early weeks, the suggestion by the Belgian ambassador in Leopoldville for a substantial peacekeeping role for his troops for a brief emergency period was immediately rejected by Ralph Bunche as incompatible with the July 14, 1960, resolution which called for the withdrawal of Belgian troops.

The United Nations Mandate

The original Security Council resolution of July 14 and the two subsequent Council resolutions during the Lumumba government, July 22 and August 9, were all supported by the United States, the Soviet Union, Argentina, Ceylon, Ecuador, Poland, and Tunisia.[18] No Council member voted against any

[18] The texts of U.N. resolutions on the Congo are found in Appendix B.

resolution, but France and Britain abstained in the first vote and France in the third. The wide support for the Congo Force was demonstrated by the General Assembly resolution of September 20, 1960, which endorsed the three earlier Council resolutions by a vote of 70 to 0, with the Soviet bloc, France, and the Union of South Africa abstaining.

The July 14 resolution, which was never superseded but only supplemented by subsequent resolutions, authorized the Secretary-General to provide the Congolese Central Government with military assistance until its own "national security forces may be able, in the opinion of the Government" to meet fully their tasks. The Council also called upon Belgium to withdraw its troops. It rejected proposed Soviet amendments which would have condemned Belgian actions as "armed aggression," insisted on the "immediate withdrawal" of Belgian troops, and restricted U.N. military aid to that which could be provided by African states.

The July 22 resolution called upon Belgium "to implement speedily" the withdrawal of its troops and requested all states "to refrain from any action which might undermine the territorial integrity and the political independence" of the Congo. The August 9 resolution addressed itself to the problem of Katanga and called upon Belgium to "withdraw immediately its troops" from Katanga and declared that "the entry of the United Nations force" into Katanga was "necessary." It also reaffirmed that the U.N. Force would not "in any way intervene in or be used to influence the outcome of any internal conflict, constitutional or otherwise."

With two major peacekeeping objectives—to restore and maintain law and order to prevent unilateral intervention—and with two major nonsecurity objectives—to restore economic viability and political stability—the U.N. effort was launched. Later, the security objectives were spelled out to include the prevention of civil war, the control and pacification of tribal conflicts, and the maintenance of national unity and territorial integrity.

Constraints on the Force

A distinction should be made between the sweeping objectives of the United Nations presence in the Congo and the specific functions of the U.N. Force. The "complete restoration of law and order," to use the language of the July 22, 1960, resolution, is a fundamental goal of any government. No outside agency subject to the consent of a weak, and at times virtually nonexistent, host government could be expected to achieve this aim, especially in a situation as chaotic as the Congo. The United Nations did not have the authority of an occupying power, nor was it a substitute government. It required not only the consent of the host government, but also the consent and support of the states that provided troops, money, and logistical support.

In addition to these inherent limitations, the operations of the Force were often further limited by an attitude of noncooperation and even hostility on the part of certain Congolese political and military officials toward U.N. officers and proposals. A certain amount of tension and hostility between any host government and an outside agency seeking to assist it is to be expected; but, in the case of the Congo, there were particular points of irritation which exacerbated the expected level of tension between two such parties.

On the basis of his understanding of the legal competence of the United Nations, the nature of the mandate, and the situation in the Congo, Hammarskjold developed a series of ground rules defining the relationship between the Congolese Central Government and the UNF, which he regarded as a "temporary security force" deployed with the "consent" of the host state. In formulating six major operating principles, the Secretary-General drew upon the experience of the U.N. Emergency Force (UNEF) in Gaza, his only precedent, which proved to be useful, although not entirely adequate, for the more complex Congo problem.[19]

[19] U.N. Security Council, Fifteenth Year, *Official Records,* Supplement for July, Aug., Sept., 1960, Doc. S/4389 (July 18, 1960), pp. 16-20.

First, the Force must be under the "exclusive command" of the Secretary-General who was accountable only to the Security Council. It could not take orders from the host government and could not act "either in competition with . . . or in cooperation with" the government. U.N. operations "must be separate and distinct from activities of any national authorities."

Second, the United Nations must not interfere in the internal affairs of the Congo, that is, not become a party "in internal conflicts." U.N. troops could not be used "to enforce any specific political solution." This principle was implied in the first resolution and made explicit in the August 9, 1960, resolution.

Third, the Force must have "freedom of movement" throughout the Congo necessary to accomplish its mission. This principle was also mentioned in the July 29 agreement between the United Nations and the Congolese government.[20] The struggle to exercise fully this right in Katanga persisted until January 1963.

Fourth, U.N. troops should use force "only in self-defense," and not exercise "any *initiative* in the use of armed force."

Fifth, the composition of the Force must be decided by the Secretary-General, although the views of the host state should be taken into account. Hammarskjold expressed a preference for requesting troops from African countries first, but also emphasized the principle of universality.

Sixth, national units in the U.N. Force should take orders only from the U.N. command and not from their governments. A situation of "dual loyalty" would deprive the operation of its "international character."

The ground rules prohibiting the UNF from interfering in internal affairs and from initiating military action acknowledged the inhibitions under which any nonsanctions, peacekeeping effort must operate. The insistence on independence from national control, freedom of movement, and loyalty to the

---

[20] U.N. Doc. S/4389, Add. 5 (July 29, 1960). See Appendix C.

U.N. command provided the United Nations, in theory, with a considerable degree of authority. In practice, however, freedom of movement in Katanga was frustrated and the authority of the U.N. commander was restricted by conditions placed upon him by states contributing troops and in other ways. His independence from national control, for example, did not give the U.N. commander the authority to discipline a soldier guilty of a crime; his only course was to hand the soldier over to his national unit commander for discipline.

Composition of the Force

Mr. Hammarskjold developed five guidelines in determining the composition of the Force. *First,* he insisted that he alone had the authority to decide what states should be invited to contribute units, though he should take fully into account the views of the host state. *Second,* units from permanent members of the Security Council should be excluded. *Third,* assistance should be sought first from "sister African nations, as an act of African solidarity." *Fourth,* "this natural reliance on regional solidarity" should be qualified by the essential "element of universality." *Fifth,* units from any state "possibly having a special interest in the situation" should be excluded.[21]

As matters developed there was soon a clash between the principle of "regional solidarity" and the principle of disinterestedness. For reasons of proximity and political ambition, some of the African states were the least disinterested. Motivated by the expansionist policy of President Kwame Nkrumah, Ghana sent a delegation to Leopoldville even before the Congo requested U.N. assistance. Nkrumah, becoming increasingly "anti-colonialist" and pan-Africanist, looked

[21] U.N. Doc. S/4389.

upon Lumumba as a protégé who would help bring the Congo into the African political federation he was attempting to forge. President Sekou Touré of Guinea was a rival aspirant for pan-African leadership in spite of the tenuous union between Guinea and Ghana. The other African donor states had less pronounced and less direct interests in the Congo, but each was intent on enhancing its prestige among the emerging states to the south. North of the Sahara, Tunisia and Ethiopia tended to be pro-Western and each pursued policies compatible with those of the United States toward the Congo. The United Arab Republic, Morocco, and Mali were neutralist and their position tended to support the Soviet strategy in the Congo. Hammarskjold's alleged hostility toward Lumumba drew condemnation from Russia and severe criticism from some the neutralist donors. Early in 1961, the United Arab Republic, Mali, and Guinea withdrew their troops over this issue.

Hammarskjold never intended to confine his recruiting to the African states. As early as July 17, 1960, he made clear in his first report that the principle of universality and the requirements for speed and special capabilities compelled him to seek aid from Asian and Western states. He had already authorized, with the consent of Stockholm, the transfer of the Swedish U.N. battalion in Gaza to the Congo. He had also appealed to the United States and Britain for aircraft and heavy equipment; and to Canada, Sweden, and Norway for specialized military personnel. By July 17, too, food was being flown into Leopoldville by American, British, Canadian, and Soviet planes. India had also been asked to provide a "senior officer as military adviser" to the Secretary-General for the Congo operation. In response, Brigadier General Indar Jit Rikhye was sent to New York as Hammarskjold's military adviser on the Congo operation.[22]

---

[22] Subsequently, this position was made permanent under the title, Military Adviser to the Secretary-General, and not tied to any specific peacekeeping operation.

Support for the U.N. Mission

With a broad and vague mandate and with severely limited authority, the Secretary-General approached the novel and ever-changing challenge in the Congo, constantly assailed by conflicting political pressures inside and outside the country. Hammarskjold was aware that his mandate did not provide the United Nations with the authority and means necessary for the accomplishment of the far-reaching goals of the mission. As events unfolded, he was pressured on the one side to act more vigorously, and on the other to refrain from "interfering in internal affairs." Resisting these pressures, Hammarskjold pursued a remarkably consistent course. Using UNEF as a precedent and guided by the Charter, he attempted to be an impartial international civil servant. When caught in policy conflicts, he repeatedly sought clarification of the mandate from the Security Council or the General Assembly, but often with little success. Not only were U.N. members divided between proponents and opponents of the Congo mission, but the supporters themselves did not agree on the application of the mandate to specific problems in the Congo. They often agreed only that something ought to be done. Under these difficult and unprecedented circumstances, including the chaos and confusion in the Congo itself, Hammarskjold developed a careful and elaborate legal basis for his policy in the Congo. In September 1960, he created a Congo Advisory Committee, made up of representatives of states contributing troop contingents. This committee functioned until the withdrawal of the UNF in 1964.

There was almost complete concurrence between America's desire for stability in central Africa and the U.N. resolutions emphasizing law and order in the Congo. For this basic reason, the United States provided the strongest and most consistent support of any state: support expressed in diplomatic, financial, and logistical terms. In spite of differences, sometimes more than trivial, between Hammarskjold's view and the American view as to the appropriate means for the U.N. operation, their positions were usually not far apart.

The other supporters, which included many Asian and African states, the Scandinavian countries, Canada, and Ireland, can be said to have constituted, together with the United States, an ad hoc working coalition based upon a shared interest in preventing the Congo situation from disintegrating further. Many of these states had sharply conflicting interests on other matters. By virtue of its power and its active participation, the United States was the most influential member of this coalition. Since the provision of troops, materiel, or airlift effort was voluntary, the United States—or any other cooperating state for that matter—could have withdrawn such support at any time. If Washington *had* withdrawn its political, logistical, and financial support, the U.N. mission would have collapsed. U.S. financial support included both the provision of ready cash and the advancement of credit.

Two of America's closest allies, Britain and France, were cool to the U.N. operation from the beginning. France was consistently but quietly hostile and, in keeping with its general attitude toward peacekeeping operations, had provided no financial support. Britain paid her quota and assisted with airlift in the initial phase, but did not cooperate fully with subsequent efforts of the UNF to deal with the Katanga problem. Portugal and South Africa were openly hostile. The Soviet Union supported the operation in the beginning and contributed some airlift, but it soon became antagonistic and intervened unilaterally in direct opposition to the Security Council resolutions. In the General Assembly debate, September 17-21, 1960, the U.S. delegate condemned the Soviet Union for dispatching to the Congo as follows:

> . . . hundreds of so-called technicians—whose character may be judged by the fact that only a few days ago the Congolese authorities ordered these men to leave the Congo. Meanwhile, nearly two dozen Soviet transport aircraft and one hundred Soviet trucks appeared in the Congo, not to participate in the United Nations program, not to put themselves under the United Nations author-

ities there, but to promote strife and bloodshed between Congolese tribes and factions.[23]

The Ambiguous Belgian Position

The first Security Council resolution with respect to the Congo called for the withdrawal of Belgian troops. Subsequent resolutions demanded the quick repatriation of remaining Belgian forces, especially from Katanga. As the chief specified target of the Council mandate, Brussels was naturally apprehensive about the mission. At the international level, however, the Belgian government from the beginning endorsed the objectives of the peacekeeping effort; but in Katanga itself some Belgian officials advised Tshombe to obstruct Hammarskjold's plans to establish a military presence there.

Katangan secession was widely assumed to have been inspired and engineered by the Belgian government. This assumption is not wholly correct. On July 11, 1960, the day Tshombe declared Katanga independent, the Belgian Foreign Minister, Pierre Wigny, informed the United States, Britain, France, West Germany, and the Netherlands that for many reasons his government was opposed to Tshombe's "intrigues." He feared that the immediate reaction to the announced secession would endanger European lives elsewhere in the Congo. He said it would inflame the negotiating atmosphere for determining the relation between Katanga and the Central Government. "Long-term secession would compromise the economic vitality of the rest of the Congo which would fall prey to Communism." At the same time, in response to Tshombe's request to Belgium to continue its technical, financial, and military aid, and to reestablish public order and security, Wigny said that Belgian metropolitan troops would "remain on the spot as long as necessary." He added: "Any interventions [in Katanga] would be unnecessary and would risk increasing the con-

[23] U.S. Participation in the U.N.: Report by the President to the Congress for the Year 1960 (U.S. Department of State Publication 7341, March 1962), p. 50.

fusion."[24] The reference to intervention reflected the fear of possible Rhodesian action. Tshombe had threatened the day before to solicit the help of the Federation's Prime Minister, Sir Roy Welensky.

Belgian troops continued to maintain order in Katanga until they were officially withdrawn in September 1960. After that, 114 Belgian officers were seconded to the Katanga regime to direct Tshombe's gendarmerie.[25]

During the first ninety days of the peacekeeping operation— and thereafter for that matter—a number of Belgian nationals, including some diplomatic officials, served as political advisers to Tshombe. Some of these Belgians, supported by the great majority of their fellow countrymen living in Katanga, advised him to obstruct efforts by Hammarskjold to establish a U.N. military presence in Katanga.

Was this conflict between the Belgian position as expressed at the international level by the Foreign Minister, and as actually practiced in Katanga, a product of calculated duplicity as frequently charged? Evidence suggests that the inconsistency was rooted largely in the weakness and division within the government of Prime Minister Gaston Eyskens. The Foreign Ministry spoke with one voice, while the Defense Ministry and the Ministry of African Affairs, both of which had more direct influence in Katanga, often spoke with a different voice. The latter two ministries, or at least their leaders at that time, had a deep stake in preserving Katanga as a going concern, even if it meant disaster for the rest of the Congo. They and other Belgians sought the downfall of Prime Minister Lumumba. While these ministries were not mere puppets of the financial concerns with investments in Katanga, they had a shared interest in protecting Belgian life

[24] CRISP, Congo: 1960, Vol. II, prepared by J. Gérard-Libois and Benoit Verhaegen (Les Dossiers du CRISP, 1961), pp. 719 and 721.

[25] In the "Second Progress Report to the Secretary-General from His Special Representative in the Congo," Rajeshwar Dayal wrote: "As of October 31 [1960], there remained . . . 231 Belgian nationals (114 officers and 117 of other ranks) in the Katangese gendarmerie and 58 Belgian officers in the police." United Nations Review, Vol. 7 (December 1960), p. 27.

and property there. This interest was intensified by the fear that the rest of the Congo might disintegrate into complete chaos. The pro-Katanga forces, both within the Congo and outside, were more interested in the continued prosperity of Katanga than in creating a united Congo in which all the inhabitants, African and European, could enjoy both prosperity and political rights. The Foreign Minister and some other Belgian officials wanted to be responsive to the Council resolutions. All Belgians were justifiably concerned with protecting Belgian lives and property throughout the Congo.

The pro-Katanga forces were not united by the single objective of an independent state. Some Katanga supporters, some of the time, pursued this goal, but what they really wanted was sufficient autonomy for Katanga to protect the financial investments there, to keep a large proportion of its tax revenue in Katanga, and to administer its own internal security apparatus. A nominal federation of Congo provinces which would have guaranteed this great degree of autonomy would no doubt have satisfied Tshombe and most of his supporters, but such a loose structure would hardly have been compatible with a united and viable Congo.

It was precisely these powerful pro-Katanga pressures expressed in Brussels and London, as well as in Elisabethville, that split the weak Brussels government and made it impossible for it to be consistent. The situation did not materially change until the stronger coalition government of Prime Minister Théo Lefèvre and Foreign Minister Paul-Henri Spaak took over on May 10, 1961, a most significant turning point in Belgium's relations with the Congo and with the United Nations. Even then, it took some time before the deep inconsistencies in the official Belgian position were resolved.

The Deployment of the U.N. Force

Before the first U.N. soldier arrived, the Congo had become an arena of the Cold War as well as the battlefield between

the various shades of "colonialists" and "anti-colonialists."
The Soviet bloc and the radical African leaders supported
Lumumba's increasingly strident anticolonialism, as well as his
advocacy of a strong central government and his opposition to
secession.[26] As Lumumba became more and more anti-Belgian
and anti-American, Washington opposed him, but continued
to support the goal of a united Congo and the Secretary-
General's moderate approach to the whole problem.

One day after the July 14 resolution was adopted, the first
troops for the U.N. Force arrived in the Congo. These included 770 Ghanaians transported by British planes and 593
Tunisians transported by U.S. Air Force C-130 aircraft from
Tunis. A month later the U.N. Force totalled more than 14,000
men from twenty-four states, including the following numbers per country: Morocco, 3,250; Ethiopia, 2,547; Tunisia,
2,427; Ghana, 2,389; Ireland, 1,317; Guinea, 744; Sweden,
628; Mali, 574; Sudan, 390; Liberia, 225; Canada, 164; and
India, 73. The Secretary-General had also accepted offers of
troops from Indonesia and the United Arab Republic.[27] By
August 10, the United States had airlifted 9,213 troops and
2,334 tons of equipment to the Congo in an operation which
was to set a record in terms of total miles as "the greatest
single airlift ever carried out by any country at any time."[28]
On September 2, the Force numbered 16,082. There were
units from fourteen states, ranging in size from 173 men to
3,259 men; specialized military personnel were also sent from
an additional twelve countries.

Under the circumstances this is an impressive record, but
the transport and deployment of these troops was beset with

[26] Robert C. Good identifies three approaches among African leaders—radical,
moderate, and conservative. See his "The Congo Crisis: A Study of Post-
Colonial Politics," in Laurence W. Martin (ed.), Neutralism and Nonalignment
(Praeger, 1962), pp. 47-63.

[27] United Nations Review, Vol. 7 (September 1960), p. 8.

[28] This statement covered the period from the beginning of the operation to
December 31, 1961. See U.S. Participation in the U.N.: 1961 (U.S. Department
of State Publication 7413, August 1962), p. 87. The report adds that the Congo
airlift was accomplished "without a single fatal accident."

confusion and inefficiency because of the novelty of the situation, the necessity for speed, the lack of a relevant precedent, and the lack of preparation by the United Nations, the donor states, or the Congo for such an operation. The Secretariat had had to start from scratch. It had no standing force, no earmarked troops, no stockpiles of weapons or equipment, no logistical structure, no communications system, no independent intelligence capability, no contingency planning, virtually no treasury, and no assured source of funds. Its mandate was vague and the problems it confronted were distressingly complex. The Secretariat did have three assets: the experience of UNEF, the broad mandate conferred by the Council resolutions, and a skillful and politically astute Secretary-General supported by an able staff of top aides committed to an impartial peacekeeping operation.

One incident dramatized the problems of quick improvisation. The newly designated Force commander, Major General Carl von Horn of Sweden, then head of the U.N. Truce Supervisory Organization in Jerusalem, waited impatiently for five days for a tardy plane chartered by the United Nations to take him and several other officers to the Congo. Finally, he landed in Leopoldville in a U.S. plane on July 18, three days after his first troops had arrived.[29]

Within days there were thousands of troops of different nationalities who had to be deployed over the vast area of the Congo without adequate communications or transportation. The rail and water route from the Congo's Atlantic port of Matadi to Elisabethville, for example, is 1,728 miles. An internal air transport system had to be improvised. Medical services and a rations system had to be organized without benefit of planning. A command structure from New York to Leopoldville and from Leopoldville to the field had to be set up overnight. It was a general's nightmare. Dr. Bunche, the temporary UNF commander until von Horn's arrival, said on

[29] Interview with Major General von Horn in Beirut, Lebanon, December 6, 1963.

August 21 that there was much room for valid criticism of the
UNF in the Congo. It had to be quickly improvised from
nothing; its military personnel had been recruited from twenty-
six different countries; it had encountered internal conflicts,
including serious intertribal warfare; and it had been dropped
into the midst of a country and people who were totally unprepared by experience and psychology to understand it and
to appreciate its functions and real worth.[30]

Functions of the Force

Under these extenuating circumstances, the UNF deployed
units in strategic areas, except for Katanga, and established a
degree of order. In addition to the task of organizing itself,
the Force had four primary functions: (1) to replace Belgian
soldiers who were currently maintaining the peace in several
areas, mainly in Leopoldville and Katanga; (2) to curb and
serve as a substitute for unreliable ANC troops who were a continuing cause of disorder; (3) to help transform the ANC into
a reliable force; and (4) to establish its own freedom of movement, particularly in Katanga.

The replacement of Belgian troops proved to be the least
difficult task. On July 16, 1960, Bunche deployed U.N. units
at the radio and power stations and in the European sector of
Leopoldville. He cooperated closely with Belgian authorities
in their common desire to maintain order in the capital city.
In a smooth four-day operation, a multinational unit replaced
Belgian soldiers in the city. Bunche also sent units to Stanleyville, Matadi, Thysville, and Coquilhatville.

To the consternation of Lumumba, the U.N. command made
no attempt to expel the Belgian troops forcibly either from
Katanga or from the Kitona and Kamina bases, held under the
unratified Treaty of Friendship. But, by August 23, the United Nations had peacefully taken over temporary administra-

[30] U.N. Security Council, Fifteenth Year, *Official Records,* Supplement for
July, Aug., Sept., 1960, Doc. S/4451, p. 113.

tion of the two bases, retaining an unspecified number of Belgian technicians in a civilian capacity to maintain them. By early September, all Belgian troops (including the 1,100 Belgian officers of the ANC) had officially left the Congo, except for the 231 officers and other ranks who remained in violation of the Council resolutions to serve in Tshombe's gendarmerie in Katanga. These men were repatriated one year later.

The task of taming, reorganizing, and training the unreliable Congolese army (ANC) was a far more difficult matter than effecting the withdrawal of Belgian troops. Brussels was responsive to persuasion and pressure. Not so were Lumumba and certain other Congolese civilian and military officials. Lumumba wanted the UNF to supplement the ANC units under his control, not to substitute for them, and certainly not to disarm them. The Secretary-General, of course, refused to take orders from the Prime Minister. The UNF sought to restore order in key areas and its very presence had some deterrent effect on the behavior of ill-disciplined and irresponsible ANC units.

With instructions to use force only in self-defense, the UNF was severely limited in the measures it could take to deal with immediate challenges to order. It was equally limited in its authority to retrain or reorganize the ANC against the will of the Congolese leaders. An incident on August 18, 1960, at the Leopoldville airport dramatically illustrated the gulf between the ultimate objective of creating a reliable Congolese security force and the limited authority of the United Nations for accomplishing this objective. On that day, Congolese soldiers surrounded a United Nations C-119 plane, interrogated the crew, and manhandled four Canadian members of the UNF, in an unprovoked but possibly politically motivated assault. The Congolese accused the Canadians of being Belgian paratroopers. After some delay, the U.N. Ghanaian unit guarding the airport succeeded in releasing the Canadians.[31] Hammarskjold lodged a strong protest with the Leopoldville govern-

[31] CRISP, *Congo: 1960*, Vol. II prepared by J. Gérard-Libois and Benoit Verhaegen (Les Dossiers du CRISP, 1961), p. 620.

ment and, at the same time, criticized the Ghanaian unit for its passive behavior in face of the assault. The incident and Hammarskjold's rebuke to the Ghanaian soldiers precipitated a sharp exchange between Major General H. T. Alexander, the British commander of the Ghanaian contingent, and Dr. Bunche, then the Secretary-General's special representative in the Congo. This revealed the dilemma the United Nations faced in dealing with the problem of disciplining and training the ANC.

Major General Alexander, in a report forwarded to Hammar-skjold by President Kwame Nkrumah of Ghana, acknowledged the fact of the unfortunate airport incident, but strongly repudiated "any criticisms of Ghanaian officers and men."[32] Noting this was but one of many similar cases of ANC atroc-ities and indiscipline, Alexander said the "immediate and also long-term possibility of getting the country back to normal hinges on the retraining and disciplining" of the Congolese army. The first task, he added, was to disarm the ANC, implying that force should be used if persuasion failed. He said, however, that he together with only two Ghanaian officers had completely and peacefully disarmed the ANC units in Leopoldville, suggesting that a general policy of disarming Congolese would meet with little or no resistance. Alexander also criticized Major General von Horn, the UNF commander, for failing to give specific orders to his contingents, and for his unwillingness to "exercise any military authority at all, thus putting Ghanaian and other U.N. troops in an impossible position." He added: "The situation is not irretrievable, but it will certainly be hopeless unless something drastic is done" to deal with the ANC problem.

Alexander was not the only U.N. commander who disarmed Congolese troops. In Luluabourg, 3,000 ANC soldiers laid down their arms as Tunisian UNF troops moved in. Though this experience was repeated elsewhere, it is difficult to ascertain the extent of this passive disarmament. It was widespread

[32] U.N. Security Council, Fifteenth Year, *Official Records,* Supplement for July, Aug., Sept., 1960, Doc. S/4445 (August 19, 1960), pp. 101-102.

enough, however, to evoke criticism from the Russians who considered such disarmament inimical to the interests of Lumumba.[33]

The Leopoldville government sometimes encouraged ANC units to lay down their arms as the UNF moved in, and sometimes took the opposite position. Inconsistency on this point reflected the general chaos and diffusion of authority. Lumumba wanted troops loyal to him to retain their arms, while he favored the disarmament of hostile units and those of doubtful loyalty.

Dr. Bunche took strong exception to the General's interpretation of U.N. authority. Though there was "much room for valid criticism" of the UNF, he said, Alexander's criticisms were unjustified because he did not understand that the UNF was a "peace force, not a fighting force;" that it could use arms only in self-defense; and that U.N. troops had to avoid getting into the "extreme position of having to shoot Congolese."[34] UNF commanders at all levels, he added, have been instructed to use weapons only in "cases of great and sudden emergency and for the purpose of self-defense. In such cases, the commander on the spot will ensure that the greatest care and control are used." Bunche cited a directive of the U.N. command which said: "Firing, even in self-defense, should be resorted to only in extreme instances. Any effort to disarm members of the UNF is to be regarded as a legitimate cause for self-defense."

On the difficult problem of disarming and training the unruly ANC, Bunche insisted that nothing could be done without the cooperation of the Central Government. Leopoldville's criticism of the UNF for "disarming" units of the ANC, he said, was unjust because any surrender of arms by Congolese troops on "the arrival of elements of the UNF" had been "purely voluntary." Although "a reorganized and disci-

---

[33] U.N. Security Council, Fifteenth Year, *Official Records*, 885th Meeting (August 8, 1960), p. 17.

[34] U.N. Security Council, Fifteenth Year, *Official Records*, Supplement for July, Aug., Sept., 1960, Doc. S/4451 (August 21, 1960), pp. 113-15.

plined Congolese National Army is a most, perhaps the most, vital problem," the "way of force offers no possibility for an international body operating in a sovereign country at the invitation of that country." Bunche added:

> The United Nations in the Congo has neither sought to replace the Congo Government nor to make it a captive. The UNF is in the Congo as a friend and partner, not as an army of occupation. It has studiously avoided any suggestion of replacing in any way the former colonial administration.[35]

Bunche's legally correct and authoritative view prevailed and there was no systematic effort on the part of the UNF to disarm ANC units, though his words did not dispel the suspicions of certain Congolese leaders who tended to look upon the UNF as an occupying army. The passive disarmament which had occurred during July and early August 1960 was short-lived and the process was actually reversed in mid-August when the U.N. command gave in to Lumumba's demand that certain disarmed units be permitted to recover their weapons. As Alexander and others had predicted, the failure to disarm or discipline the Congolese troops had fateful consequences. The United Nations intervened in the first instance primarily because of the irresponsibility of the ANC, and the continuing presence of the UNF was required in part by the persistent irresponsibility of most of the ANC units, some of which were not better than marauding bands. Had the ANC been disarmed and kept disarmed, there would have been no domestic military support for contending political factions which continued to tear the country apart. The restoration of order and the creation of a unified national government would have been less difficult.

Nearly all competent observers, including Bunche and Alexander, were agreed on the desirability of disarming the ANC, but they differed on the feasibility of doing so, given the UNF's limited authority. In retrospect, however, it appears that disarmament without coercion might have been possible

---

[35] *Ibid.*

if the Secretary-General had given the highest priority to this objective, if it had been vigorously pursued at the diplomatic level in New York and the political level in Leopoldville, and if all U.N. commanders had been instructed to engage in active persuasion toward this end. Evidence suggests that the physical presence of a competent military unit commanded by white officers might well have been sufficient in the great majority of cases to achieve passive disarmament.

Disarmament by persuasion would have required speed and skill under a clear directive. In the chaos and confusion of the first six weeks, the hastily deployed UNF was preoccupied with many pressing tasks and the best, and perhaps only, opportunity to develop and implement an effective plan slipped by. Given the weaknesses and contradictions within the Central Government and the attitude of suspicion toward the United Nations on the part of Lumumba and some Congolese military officers, perhaps even a concerted diplomatic effort to persuade Lumumba through the good offices of other African leaders would not have succeeded in convincing him that the passive disarmament of his unreliable troops was in the best interest of the Congo. On the other hand, given the chaos, effective disarmament might well have been accomplished without Lumumba's consent.

Lumumba vs. the United Nations

From the first days of the United Nations presence, Lumumba had difficulty getting along with the U.N., U.S., and Belgian officials in Leopoldville. By the time of their arrival, he had already rather fully identified himself with radical African spokesmen whose interpretation of "colonialism" and "Western imperialism" were virtually indistinguishable from those of the Soviet bloc. The bloc supported Lumumba openly while Communist agents in the Congo supported him covertly. Lumumba was described by a high American official as "the most effective political organizer and rabble-rouser" in the

Congo, "intelligent, articulate, and politically sophisticated, and at the same time unscrupulous and untrustworthy." Further, he was said to have been a drug addict and afflicted with serious psychological problems.

It was inevitable that Lumumba and Hammarskjold would soon clash over the proper role of the UNF, especially as it related to secessionist Katanga. It must be remembered that Belgian troops were not withdrawn from Katanga until September 1960 and, before they left, Tshombe's gendarmes were strengthened and trained under the direction of Belgian officers. Elisabethville persisted in its refusal to admit U.N. troops, and thwarted Bunche's abortive effort to introduce a token military presence on August 4, 1960.

Exasperated by this situation, Lumumba repeatedly demanded that the UNF immediately expel the Belgian troops in Katanga and compel Tshombe to end his secession. He insisted that the U.N. troops enter Katanga by force, alone or in a joint operation with his ANC units. This Hammarskjold could not do without violating virtually every one of his Council-backed ground rules, to say nothing of the constraints placed upon him by the states providing units. Caught between the demands of Lumumba, reinforced by repeated appeals from the Soviet Union for U.N. intervention in his behalf and the intransigence of Tshombe supported by his Belgian advisers and officers, the Secretary-General moved slowly and carefully, trying not to take sides with either camp.

Hammarskjold took his dilemma to the Security Council on August 8, 1960. How could the UNF implement its mandate without entering Katanga and how could it enter Katanga without violating its limited authority, which excluded the use of force except in self-defense? Since Hammarskjold was not prepared to surrender his objective of freedom of movement and since there was little chance of increasing the authority of the UNF, he announced that he would attempt to persuade Lumumba and Tshombe that a peaceful entry of a small unit into Katanga would not prejudice the outcome of the political struggle between them. Invoking Article 40 of the Charter, he said he could not use the entry of the UNF as a device to force Katanga to submit to the control of the Central Government. Such control was precisely what Lumumba wanted and Tshombe feared. Hammarskjold insisted that the internal political conflict be settled peacefully and said the United Nations would attempt to create conditions that would contribute toward that end.

The Council supported Hammarskjold's view. The August 9, 1960, resolution declared the entry into Katanga necessary and reaffirmed that the Force would not be a party to any internal disputes, thus paving the way for its peaceful entry.[36] On August 12, Hammarskjold, accompanied by Deputy UNF Commander General Ben Hammou Kettani of Morocco and Brigadier General Rikhye, personally escorted an advance contingent of 300 Swedish troops into Elisabethville to replace Belgian units. Within a week, U.N. troops occupied several locations in the province. Belgian troop withdrawal was begun, but the United Nations had established "freedom of movement" only in limited areas by the end of September.

All this was too snail-paced for Lumumba who made a secret deal for a shipment of Soviet military supplies and technicians to use against the secessionists, especially Tshombe. By the time Lumumba's August 27 ill-organized invasion of Katanga was launched, one hundred Russian trucks, complete with parts and repair crews, had been unloaded at Matadi. Within the next few days, eleven IL-14 transport planes were in Lumumba's service.[37] President Eisenhower said this flagrant violation of the Security Council resolutions was motivated solely by Russia's "political designs in Africa."

Constantly in conflict with Hammarskjold over the role of the UNF, Lumumba insisted that all white troops leave the

---

[36] The resolution also specifically invoked Articles 25 and 49 of the Charter which placed a mandatory responsibility upon member states to "carry out the decisions of the Security Council." This reference was addressed to Belgium and other states that were directly or indirectly assisting Tshombe in his defiance of the United Nations. The mandatory character of this paragraph did not apply to the providing of troops for the UNF which were made available on a voluntary basis.

[37] U.S. Participation in the U.N., 1960, op. cit., p. 50.

Congo and be replaced by Africans. He called the Secretary-General a Belgian "puppet" and said the Central Government had "lost confidence" in him. When Hammarskjold refused to permit the UNF to become an obedient instrument of Lumumba's will, the Prime Minister demanded its withdrawal.

A strict legal interpretation of the July 14, 1960, resolution would have given the host state authority to end the U.N. military presence at the pleasure of the Central Government, but subsequent political developments modified the original legal situation. The July 22 resolution—and the debate preceding its adoption—established a connection between the maintenance of law and order within the Congo and the maintenance of international peace, mainly because it was recognized that the Soviet bloc was exploiting internal weakness by unilateral intervention. This relationship between internal order and international peace was made more explicit in the August 9, 1960, resolution in which the Security Council invoked Articles 25 and 49, thus obligating member states to cooperate with the Council resolutions. The Congo, too, although not yet formally a member of the United Nations, was morally obligated to abide by decisions of the Council under the "good faith" clause of the July 29 agreement between the Secretary-General and the Congolese government. That agreement stated that the Central Government "will be guided, in good faith, by the fact that it has requested military assistance from the United Nations and by its acceptance of the resolutions of the Security Council of 14 and 22 July 1960."[38] Taking these factors into account, one analyst has concluded that the Congolese government "could not by unilateral action decide that the threat was over or that measures taken by the Council should be terminated." He is of the opinion that the Security Council alone was legally competent to determine these matters, although it would obviously have to take into account the views of the Central Government.[39]

---

[38] U.N. Security Council, Fifteenth Year, *Official Records*, Supplement for July, Aug., Sept., 1960, Doc. S/4389, Add. 5. See Appendix C.

[39] E. M. Miller, "Legal Aspects of the United Nations Action in the Congo," *American Journal of International Law*, Vol. 55 (January 1961), p. 15.

Lumumba's conniving with the Soviet bloc, his refusal to accept a disinterested status for the UNF, and his intemperate tactics set him at odds with the more conservative head of state, President Kasavubu. Exercising his constitutional prerogative, Kasavubu dismissed Prime Minister Lumumba on September 5 for plunging "the nation into fratricidal war." He appointed Joseph Ileo, President of the Congo Senate, as the new Prime Minister. Lumumba responded by "dismissing" Kasavubu as President. The immediate result was two contenders for the control of the Central Government, each with supporters in the international arena. Though the struggle continued for some months, this mutual dismissal marked the demise of the Lumumba government and the end of the first phase of U.N. involvement in the Congo.

General Observations

1. The fundamental problem of the Congo was internal weakness and the lack of preparation for self-government. The chaos and conflict which erupted in July 1960, after the abrupt and premature withdrawal of Belgian authority, was caused primarily by divisive internal forces and exacerbated by external parties seeking to exploit the situation for their own purposes. The crisis was not caused by Belgian "aggression." At no time during the first three months of independence or thereafter did the Security Council charge Belgium or any other state with aggression.

2. A commitment to rapid decolonization in Africa was perhaps the single most important motive for the initial interest of the Secretary-General and most of the nonaligned states in supporting U.N. military assistance to the Congo. The United States and the Soviet Union were also committed to decolonization, but they differed greatly on what it involved. To Moscow, decolonization meant expelling the Belgian military and economic presence and making the Congo safe for an extremist

regime with close ties to the Communist bloc. To Washington, decolonization meant an independent and moderate government capable of sustaining mutually beneficial relations with the West. Consequently, Washington was interested in frustrating Soviet intervention in behalf of Lumumba. The simpler anticolonialist interpretation sponsored by the Communist states and widely accepted by neutralist governments which focused almost exclusively on getting the Belgians out, continued as the dominant motive for many, if not most, of the nonaligned states throughout the four years.

3. The Congo peacekeeping effort was complicated by a profound internal conflict, the lack of a competent central government, and an executive left in disarray by departing Belgian administrators. By contrast, the problems confronted by the United Nations after the Israel-Egypt cease-fire agreement in 1956 were less difficult. In Egypt, the host state, there was no internal conflict and there was an effective government. UNEF had a clear-cut international agreement to police, and U.N. troops patrolled in a specified area from which Egyptian forces were excluded. Further, the purpose of UNEF was understood from the outset—to deter border violations by both Israel and Egypt and to serve as an international plate-glass window if there were an attack by either side.

But, in the Congo, there were two unsettled and interrelated problems. One was the continued Belgian military presence, especially in Katanga. The other and much more serious problem was the domestic struggle for power among Congolese political factions, a struggle that was considerably aggravated by the totally unreliable ANC. The Secretary-General frequently found himself in the position of having no competent government to deal with. His difficulties were further compounded by diverging interpretations as to what the UNF should do on the part of the states involved.

4. As a result of the complexity and ever-changing character of the Congo crisis and the different and sometimes conflicting

interests among the members of the Security Council, the resolutions were both vague and ambiguous. This was especially true on the question of the means the UNF was authorized to employ. This forced Hammarskjold to define the ground rules which were subsequently endorsed by the Council. Had the authority and constraints on the Force been more specifically defined in the resolutions—a theoretically desirable objective—the necessary support for dispatching a mission might have proved impossible to mobilize. The Council mandate was probably as clear as it could have been without inviting a negative vote from the United States or the Soviet Union.

5. There was an unbridgeable hiatus between the far-reaching goals of the Congo operation and the limited means legally available to the UNF. This hiatus was inevitable and was rooted in the nature of a nonsanctions, peaceful settlement force which operated with the consent of the host state. The permissible means defined in Hammarskjold's ground rules were insufficient to restore internal order and to secure the territorial integrity of the Congo. These broad objectives were beyond the capacity of any external agency which had to depend upon the cooperation of a divided and incompetent government.

6. During the first three months, there were three separate and independent military establishments on Congolese soil without a clear understanding of the relationship or primacy among them. First, there was the ANC, the mutinous Congolese army of 25,000 men which was in the process of throwing out its 1,100 Belgian officers. Second, in mid-July 1960, there were Belgian forces numbering perhaps 10,000. Third was the quickly improvised, multinational UNF which had grown to 16,000 by the end of August. In a sense, the UNF was intended to replace both the Belgians and the Congolese army, but it lacked explicit authority to expel the former or disarm the latter. The Belgian military presence was speedily withdrawn under diplomatic pressure, except for the small number of seconded officers and men who remained in

Katanga. The tense and undefined relationship between the UNF and the ANC was and continued to be one of the most perplexing problems of the entire operation. For understandable political reasons the new Congolese government was reluctant to sign status-of-forces agreements with the Secretary-General which would have placed its irresponsible troops in a subordinate position to the UNF. But if the Central Government was desperate enough to require outside military assistance, might it not have been persuaded to accept a carefully defined and temporary limitation on the role of its military establishment in the interests of restoring law and order? In retrospect, it appears that the Secretary-General might have taken a somewhat stronger hand in this direction.

Depending upon the political circumstances surrounding a U.N. peacekeeping mission, the existing military or police forces in the host state, domestic or foreign, can function in effect as an ally of the international effort, as an adversary, or as a neutral factor. In the Congo, different elements of the ANC at different times played all three roles, but in this period, Congolese troops were cast largely in neutral or adversary roles.

2

Peacekeeping
in a Political Vacuum

*By mid-September the constitutional crises had re-
sulted in the breakdown of the formal structure of
government into . . . competitive power groups headed
by the Chief of State, the Prime Minister, the Parliament and, more recently, the Army.*

RAJESHWAR DAYAL, SEPTEMBER 21, 1960

THE ABRUPT DISMISSAL of Prime Minister Lumumba
by President Kasavubu on September 5, 1960, raised the curtain
on the second act of the Congo drama. That same day, in
angry retaliation, Lumumba made three fiery speeches over
Radio Leopoldville denouncing and "dismissing" Kasavubu
and calling upon the workers and the Congolese army—the
ANC—for support. That night, faced with mounting confusion and disorder, Andrew Cordier, Hammarskjold's temporary special representative in the Congo, closed all major airports in the country to all except U.N. traffic "in the interests
of the maintenance of peace." In a related move the next day,
he temporarily closed the Leopoldville radio station. These
measures were taken to preserve order. The effect was to
block unilateral Soviet military action, contrary to the Security
Council resolutions. Specifically, the airports were closed to
prevent Soviet IL-14 planes from transporting Lumumba-
controlled troops to Leopoldville and elsewhere. After strong

46

protests from Kasavubu and Lumumba, the Leopoldville radio was returned to the Central Government on September 12. The airports were retained under U.N. control.

These fast-moving events precipitated a constitutional crisis in the Congo which lasted until August 2, 1961, when the Parliament unanimously endorsed Kasavubu's designation of Cyrille Adoula as Prime Minister. During these eleven turbulent months, there was a political vacuum in the Congo in which two factions were claiming to be the legitimate central government and various provincial leaders acknowledged no central government at all.

Under these circumstances it was impossible for the United Nations to take any initiative in the Congo whatsoever without affecting its internal affairs. Cordier's controversial actions, intended to keep order and prevent foreign intervention, had a profound impact upon the domestic struggle for the control of the Central Government. Their net effect was to frustrate the ambitions of Lumumba and his outside supporters and to further the fortunes of Kasavubu and other moderate leaders.

During this entire period, the Secretary-General sought to pursue an impartial and disinterested policy toward rival claimants. The UNF, for example, provided protection for Lumumba, Kasavubu, Tshombe, and other Congo leaders. The Secretary-General's special representative in the Congo, with the active support of U.S. and Belgian officials, tried to get the various Congolese factions to resolve their differences peaceably. But virtually everything Hammarskjold, his man in Leopoldville, or the UNF did—or did not do—antagonized one or more factions and their supporters in the larger world. Nevertheless, the Secretary-General continued to press for a unified Congo under a government acceptable to all major factions in accord with the Security Council resolutions that explicitly called for a parliamentary solution in the Congo. With this commitment to a constitutional solution, the operation had the effect of supporting the political moderates and undermining the extremists who operated by revolutionary or other unconstitutional means.

Chronology of Chaos

From September 1960 until the following August when the Congolese Parliament endorsed Prime Minister Adoula, two parallel dramas were unfolding: one in the Congo and the other at the U.N. Headquarters in New York. Both had elements of high tragedy and low comedy, and the moves by the actors in each theater impinged upon the other. A brief review of this drama is essential to an understanding of the problems and performance of the UNF in what was perhaps its most difficult period.

On September 12, just as the two rival Congo delegations arrived in New York to be seated in the United Nations, Colonel Joseph Mobutu, ANC Chief of Staff, arrested Lumumba. Two days later, Mobutu entered the political conflict by announcing an army take-over until the end of the year to "neutralize" the governments of both Lumumba and Kasavubu's choice, Joseph Ileo. Mobutu established what later became known as the "Council of Commissioners" which subsequently received Kasavubu's blessing. He expelled the Czech and Soviet diplomatic missions for interference in the Congo's affairs and also dismissed Parliament which had tended to side with Lumumba. Mobutu's actions strengthened the Kasavubu regime but obviously could not be squared legally with the Fundamental Law (*Loi Fondamentale*), the Congo's provisional constitution. Lumumba continued to claim he was the legitimate Prime Minister. He was later placed under house arrest and U.N. protection in Leopoldville.

Each rival contender in the Congo power struggle sought the sanction and the assistance of the United Nations. Hammarskjold resolved the problem by recognizing only President Kasavubu whose office, in his view, had not been compromised by the conflict. He refused to extend this mantle of legitimacy to the Council of Commissioners, consisting of young university students and graduates who had been serving as Mobutu's personal brain trust. In routine matters, the U.N. officials in the Congo transacted business with the man they "found at the head of government departments."[1] This policy of recognizing only Kasavubu was carried out on the spot by Rajeshwar Dayal of India, Hammarskjold's new special representative in Leopoldville, who said his mission was "to help but not to intervene, to advise but not to order, to conciliate but not to take sides."[2]

Hammarskjold's aloofness toward rival claimants during this period of political chaos irritated both sides. Some Western supporters of the Kasavubu-Mobutu regime suspected that the Secretary-General's posture was designed more to save the reputation of the Secretariat as an impartial body than to save the Congo. Hammarskjold was obviously trying to do both, but if he did emphasize the former objective, it was certainly understandable in light of the increasingly bitter Soviet attack against the office of the Secretary-General and Hammarskjold himself.

In the Congo, the latter part of September 1960 was characterized by the following developments: the growing antagonism of Kasavubu and Mobutu toward Ghana and Guinea because of their support for Lumumba; renewed attempts by several African states to mediate the Kasavubu-Lumumba conflict; the evacuation of Congolese troops from northern Katanga under U.N. auspices to avoid civil war; and the massacre of Baluba tribesmen, reputed to be the work of Tshombe and his men.

In the meanwhile, back in New York the Congo problem preoccupied the Security Council. But, after a period of fruitless Council debate and failure to agree on any action, a special emergency session of the General Assembly was called on September 17, 1960, at the request of the United States. On September 20, the Assembly adopted a resolution which reaffirmed previous Council actions in relation to the Congo, appealed

---

[1] U.N. General Assembly, Sixteenth Session, *Official Records*, Supplement No. 1 (*Annual Report of the Secretary-General on the Work of the Organization, 16 June, 1960, to 15 June, 1961*), Doc. A/4800, p. 20.

[2] *Ibid.*, p. 18.

to the Congolese to solve their problems by peaceful and parliamentary means, and called upon all states to refrain from providing military assistance except at the request of the Secretary-General. The vote was 70 to 0, with 11 abstentions.

This wide support for Hammarskjold's interpretation of his mandate in the Congo infuriated the Soviet Union. In his major speech in the Assembly on September 23, Khrushchev called upon Hammarskjold to resign and proposed his famous troika arrangement for administering the Secretariat. Secretary of State Christian A. Herter promptly labeled the speech a "declaration of war" against the United Nations. Khrushchev's most bitter attack against Hammarskjold came during the Assembly debate on October 3. He charged that the Secretary-General, in carrying out his Congo policy, was guilty of "arbitrary and lawless behavior," that he had "violated the elementary principles of justice," and had "supported the colonialists."[3] Khrushchev again called for the resignation of Hammarskjold and demanded that the office of a single Secretary-General be abolished in favor of a triumvirate representing the three political "camps" in the world.

The relationship between the United Nations and Leopoldville improved somewhat after the General Assembly seated the Kasavubu delegation on November 22, 1960. The vote was 53 to 24, with 19 abstentions. In this vote the United States supported Kasavubu; the Soviet bloc, Ghana, Guinea, and several other African states supported Lumumba.

On November 27, 1960, under mysterious circumstances, Lumumba escaped from Leopoldville where he had been under U.N. protection to join his supporters in Stanleyville. Four days later, he was recaptured in Kasai by Mobutu's troops, returned to Leopoldville, and imprisoned to await trial. Protesting Lumumba's arrest, the United Arab Republic, Yugoslavia, Indonesia, Morocco, Mali, and Guinea announced their intention of withdrawing their units from the UNF. This deci-

[3] U.N. General Assembly, Fifteenth Session, *Official Records*, 882nd Meeting (October 3, 1960), pp. 317-21.

sion was reaffirmed at the Casablanca conference e[
January 1961 and, by April, all these contingents had l[

At the request of the Soviet Union, the Security Counc
convened in February 1961 to consider Lumumba's ⸺.
The Council failed to pass either the resolutions proposed by
the United States or the Soviet Union and the debate was
again transferred to the General Assembly. The larger forum
was likewise split into factions over what were essentially
internal political questions in the Congo.

On February 13, 1961, the Katanga radio announced that ✓
Lumumba had been killed in an attempted escape the day
before. He had been transferred to Katanga from Leopoldville
the previous month in accordance with an agreement between
Mobutu and Tshombe.[4] In the meantime, Lumumba's lieutenant, Antoine Gizenga, had established control in Stanleyville and had secured recognition for his regime from the
Communist bloc, including China, and several of the more
militant African states: the United Arab Republic, Ghana,
Guinea, Mali, and Morocco. With this development, Mobutu
and Tshombe had a mutual interest in eliminating the challenge in Stanleyville.

Efforts Toward National Reconciliation

At the beginning of 1961, the Congo was divided into four
conflicting factions centering largely in provincial capitals sepa-
rated from each other by broad expanses of no-man's-land. It

---

[4] J. Gérard-Libois, Sécession au Katanga (Brussels: Centre de Recherche et
d'Information Socio-Politiques, 1963), pp. 164-65. (After holding sixty-six
meetings, the U.N. Commission set up to inquire into Lumumba's death reported
on November 11, 1961: "Mr. Lumumba, Mr. Okito, and Mr. Mpolo were executed by a Belgian mercenary on 17 January 1961 not far from Elisabethville,
and in all probability in the presence of certain members of the Government of
Katanga Province, namely Mr. Tshombe, Mr. Munongo, and Mr. Kibwe." U.N.
General Assembly, Seventeenth Session, Official Records, Supplement No. 1,
Doc. A/5201, p. 8.)

was a shifting and lopsided picture—Kasavubu in Leopoldville with about 7,000 troops, Gizenga in Stanleyville with about 5,500 troops, Tshombe in Elisabethville with between 5,000 and 7,000 troops, and Albert Kalonji in South Kasai with about 3,000 troops. Both Leopoldville and Stanleyville claimed national jurisdiction and campaigned for unity. Elisabethville alternately sought complete independence and membership in a loose Congo confederation. Kalonji in South Kasai operated autonomously, seeking ties first with Tshombe and then with Leopoldville. The Secretary-General and his representative in the Congo continued to pursue a policy of impartiality toward all claimants, though they had developed a mood, if not a posture, of hostility toward Tshombe on the ground that he flouted the Council resolutions and failed to keep his word on several occasions.

During this period, the American ambassador to the Congo worked closely with U.N. officials in attempting to get the Congolese factions together. In early January 1961, the U.N. Conciliation Commission, created the previous November by the Secretary-General's Congo Advisory Committee, arrived in Leopoldville.[5] Like the committee, the commission was composed of the fifteen Asian and African states with troops in the Congo. The function of the commission was to help the Congolese restore parliamentary institutions and create a government representing all major factions. The United Arab Republic, Guinea, and Mali refused to join the commission because they believed the cards were stacked against Gizenga. The former state was about to withdraw its contingent from the UNF and the latter two had already done so. Three months later, the commission issued a report endorsed by the United States and a great majority of the other U.N. members. It made the following points:

1. Representative Congolese leaders should meet to discuss "a federal form of government," but the Fundamental Law

[5] The Congo Advisory Committee, which had been established on August 23, 1960, by the Secretary-General, consisted of the Permanent Representatives of the states which had provided contingents for the United Nations Force.

should be upheld until it was amended or replaced. Parliamentary government should be established.

2. Tribal warfare and undisciplined armed groups were a serious danger.

3. Until the ANC could be reorganized and disciplined, the UNF should continue to maintain law and order. To carry out "its increased responsibilities," the UNF would have to be "strengthened to a considerable extent, both in men and modern equipment."

4. Foreign interference should be ended, especially military aid to any faction. The continued presence of "Belgian and other foreign military and paramilitary personnel, political advisers, and mercenaries" was deplored.[6]

A summit conference of Congolese leaders was held, March 6-12, 1961, in Tananarive, Malagasy Republic. The participants included Kasavubu and Tshombe, but not Gizenga, though all major political leaders had been invited. The conference agreed to form a confederation of Congo states. A second major political conference, also marred by partial representation, was held at Coquilhatville in April. It agreed that the Congo should become a "Federal Republic" of states with a single diplomatic service, a unified military force, and one currency. These two conferences contributed little to genuine national reconciliation.

Responding to the advice of the Security Council, the General Assembly, and U.N. officials in the Congo, Parliament was reconvened under U.N. protection on July 19, 1961, at Lovanium University on the edge of Leopoldville. The arrangements for the meeting made by U.N. officials were unusual. Armed Congolese soldiers and police were not permitted to move about in the city. During the session all members were housed in the university buildings and were permitted no contacts with the outside world. No participant was allowed "any weapons, any money, or any other negotiable instruments of

[6] *Report of the United Nations Conciliation Commission for Congo*, Doc. A/4711 (March 20, 1961).

any kind, either when entering Lovanium or upon . . . departure."

After two weeks, the diplomatic pressure to find a solution to the constitutional crisis yielded results. President Kasavubu's designation of Cyrille Adoula as Prime Minister was unanimously endorsed by both the Assembly and Senate of the Congo on August 2, 1961, ending eleven months of chaos following the dismissal of Lumumba. Though the Congo finally had a legal and widely recognized government, the government itself had no effective political or military control in many areas of the Congo and no control at all in the southern part of secessionist Katanga. From this point on, Katanga was the major problem for the new Central Government and the United Nations.

A New Mandate for the U.N. Force

The frustrations of the United Nations in dealing with the chaotic situation, especially in Katanga, developed pressures for a broader mandate. The UNF was widely criticized for its passivity, but this criticism was hardly justifiable in light of the existing constraints against using force except in self-defense. Further, the Force had no authority to apprehend mercenaries, to arrest, to release persons arrested by others, or to search or inspect for illegally imported weapons. Lacking many of the powers of a normal police force within a state, UNF commanders often felt their hands were tied. The Secretary-General was pressed to act more decisively and forcibly than his authorized ground rules permitted. In the December 1960 Council debate, several speakers called for armed UNF intervention in various factional struggles in the Congo, but Hammarskjold again pointed out that the Council mandate did not include the "enforcement" powers provided in Articles 41 and 42 of the Charter.

Because of these pressures, and Dayal's candid reporting of the deteriorating situation, Hammarskjold urged the Security

Council on February 1, 1961, to strengthen his mandate to utilize the UNF in a more effective manner to cope with continuing civil strife and the problem of foreign mercenaries. After prolonged debate, the Council on February 21 adopted a resolution by a vote of 9 to 0, with 2 abstentions, France and the Soviet Union. This authorized U.N. troops to employ "force, if necessary in the last resort," to prevent "civil war." Because of the continued presence of seconded Belgian officers and political advisers in Katanga, the Council also reaffirmed all previous resolutions and urged measures for "the immediate withdrawal of mercenaries" and "all Belgian and other foreign military and paramilitary personnel and political advisers not under the U.N. Command." It urged that the Congo armed forces be "reorganized and brought under discipline and control" in order not to exacerbate the factional struggle. Subsequently, Brussels agreed to withdraw all Belgians who were in the Congo in violation of the Security Council resolutions. Brussels also agreed to assist the United Nations in "urging the Congolese authorities to accept" the February 21 resolution. A proposed Soviet resolution (which would have condemned Belgium as an aggressor, ended the peacekeeping operation, and dismissed "D. Hammarskjold" as Secretary-General) was rejected by a lopsided 8-to-1 vote.

The new mandate to use force if necessary was highly controversial. It did not provide clear policy guidance, but broadened the area of permissible action and was thus susceptible to a variety of interpretations. It never would have received Britain's vote had not Hammarskjold reassured the Council that the new authority did not extend to any objective other than the prevention of civil war. It could not be used, he said, to impose any political solution in the Congo. It did not even give the UNF a legal right to search incoming trains or planes for mercenaries or weapons prohibited by Council resolutions. In attempting to prevent civil war, Hammarskjold emphasized, all means short of force would first be fully exploited.

In spite of its inherent limitations and Hammarskjold's interpretation, the use-of-force mandate was loudly condemned by Ileo and Tshombe, each of whom feared it might be employed against his interests. Subsequently, Kasavubu said he would accept the February 21 resolution provided the United Nations recognized the "sovereign rights" of the Congo.

Materially the "force, if necessary," authority did not make a big difference, at least in the beginning, but it did have a significant psychological and political effect. Under the new mandate, cautious steps were taken by the UNF and small precedents were set which paved the way for bolder action to be initiated in Katanga during the next period—action which the British said went well beyond Hammarskjold's original interpretation of the mandate.

The Role of Hammarskjold and Dayal

After the February 21 resolution, the U.N. operation faced the same spectrum of threats to law and order which had characterized the earlier period. The political context was even more confusing. Instead of one hostile Prime Minister, Lumumba, to deal with, U.N. authorities were confronted by three contending centers of power: Leopoldville, Stanleyville, and Elisabethville.

In New York, Hammarskjold faced seriously divided counsel in an atmosphere embittered by the announcement on February 13, 1961, of Lumumba's violent death in Katanga. The day after the announcement, the Soviet Union again demanded that the Secretary-General resign and said it would no longer recognize him as "an official of the United Nations." Ambassador Adlai E. Stevenson replied that Hammarskjold was far from being a "disembodied ghost."[7] Moscow continued to insist that Gizenga was the lawful head of the Congolese government.

The African states were sharply divided; the moderates like Tunisia, Ethiopia, and Nigeria joined the United States in

[7] *U.S. Participation in the U.N.: Report by the President to the Congress for the Year 1961* (U.S. Department of State Publication 7413, August 1962), p. 68.

supporting Hammarskjold, and the Casablanca group generally supported the Soviet-led opposition. On February 25, Tass made public a letter from Khrushchev to Prime Minister Nehru of India asking in effect for him to support the Soviet position on the Congo. Two days later, Nehru rejected the Soviet appeal and declared his support of the Congo operation and his confidence in the Secretary-General. On March 3, 1961, India offered a brigade of 4,700 men to the UNF.

This serious division among member states did not prevent Hammarskjold from acting. He would not resign, he said, unless the Security Council requested him to do so. In the meantime, he continued to carry out the Council mandate with the advice and consent of the Congo Advisory Committee. His formal consultation with the Advisory Committee and the Security Council was supplemented by continuous conversations with officials of the United States and other governments interested in the Congo problem. Though Hammarskjold's course of action was never censured by a majority of the Council or the Advisory Committee, he often had to operate without a positive consensus on specific matters, even among the supporting states. In these situations someone had to make decisions, and he made them. An active rather than a passive instrument, he frequently initiated plans and ideas and presented them, usually informally, to interested states. A man of great political insight and experience, he always carefully gauged the political limits of his support before undertaking a new course of action. Early in the Congo operation he had made clear to the Council the necessity of moving ahead in the absence of specific guidance:

> I have a right to expect guidance. That guidance can be given in many forms. But it should be obvious if the Security Council says nothing I have no other choice than to follow my conviction. . . . Implementation obviously means interpretation.[8]

Exercising initiative and guided by his understanding of the Charter and the Council resolutions, Hammarskjold utilized

[8] U.N. Security Council, Fifteenth Year, *Official Records*, 888th Meeting, Doc. S/PV. 888 (August 21, 1960), p. 21.

fully the powers of his office, recognizing at all times that his capacity to act effectively was ultimately derived from the diplomatic and material support of the coalition of states committed to the operation.

The severe problems of the peacekeeping effort, rooted in the conflict of political purposes in the Congo and the larger world, were aggravated during this period by growing strain and hostility between the Kasavubu-Mobutu government and Dayal, the officer in charge in Leopoldville, who had replaced Cordier in early September 1960.[9]

The "Dayal problem," as it came to be called, was a product of many factors: some inescapable, others of his own making. As the visible symbol of the United Nations in Leopoldville, he had to bear the onus of Hammarskjold's unpopular non-recognition policy. Further, the very presence of the UNF was an embarrassing reminder, especially to General Mobutu, of the Central Government's inability to control the ANC. Mobutu and other political leaders also regarded the UNF as an affront to the Congo's sovereignty. Criticism by U.N. officials of ANC irresponsibility, protests against Mobutu's use of Belgian military advisers in Leopoldville, and Dayal's blunt reporting of the chaos ruling the Congo all conspired to enflame the relationship between the Central Government and Dayal.

Perhaps the most important factor contributing toward Mobutu's distrust of the UNF in general and of Dayal in particular was the widely accepted belief in Leopoldville that certain Ghanaian and Guinean members of the UNF were implicated in subversive activities of a serious nature in the fall of 1960. The Kasavubu government charged that these men were involved in a plot to assassinate high Congolese officials. Whether the alleged plot could be verified by an impartial investigation is less important than the belief that such plotting was going on, combined with the fact that Ghana and

---

[9] Before May 25, 1961, the U.N. officer in charge in the Congo was known as the special representative of the Secretary-General. The U.N. civilian and military representatives in the Congo are listed in Appendix E.

Guinea supported Lumumba as the legitimate Prime Minister of the Congo.[10]

The various clashes between ANC and UNF troops heightened the existing tension between the UNF and Mobutu. In addition to the celebrated airport incident on August 18, 1960, noted in the previous chapter, there was a bizarre episode at the Congo's main Atlantic port, Matadi, on March 3, 1961. On that day, units of Mobutu's Leopoldville forces seized the U.N. garrison of Sudanese troops and forced it to surrender. Two Sudanese were killed. As a result, Sudan's moderate government which had been supporting the peacekeeping effort withdrew its contingent of 478 men. After extended negotiation, prolonged because of the tension between Dayal and Congolese authorities, unarmed UNF troops were finally permitted, on June 19, to return to Matadi. The loss of this strategic port at this time was a serious handicap for the Force in its movement of men and equipment.

The problem of what the U.N. operation should do about training the ANC was another source of friction. Both sides agreed on the ultimate objective of creating a responsible national army, but they disagreed as to how it should be done. In early 1961, Dayal presented a plan to disarm ANC units as a first step toward reorganization. It was rejected by Mobutu and Foreign Minister Justin Bomboko on February 4. On April 17, President Kasavubu said his government would cooperate with the United Nations in the reorganization of the ANC, but little was accomplished, primarily because of continued tension between Dayal and Mobutu.

Dayal was widely believed to have favored the Lumumba-Gizenga cause and to have given at least tacit support to pro-Lumumba forces. He was also regarded as strongly anti-Belgian.

In addition to these points of tension, many observers re-

---

[10] For a brief summary of the role of contingents from Ghana and Guinea, see Edwin S. Munger's Report of October 1960, "Conflict in the Congo: External Pressures," in *Africa Field Reports: 1952-1961* (Cape Town: C. Struck, 1961), pp. 205-208. See also AP dispatch, "Mobutu Accuses U.N. of Backing Coup Plot," *Washington Post and Times Herald,* Nov. 9, 1960.

ported that Dayal had a style and manner which irritated the Congolese as well as Western diplomats in Leopoldville. His less-than-diplomatic frankness was a source of particular annoyance. In a conversation with Mobutu, for example, he once referred to the ANC as "armed rabble," which hurt because it was all too true. He was frequently accused of being "arrogant." Without making a final assessment, it would appear that the "Dayal problem" was a compound of a very difficult situation and a personality which rubbed many people the wrong way, including the Congolese leaders.

It should be remembered that the Congo in those days was a political snake pit in which U.N. officers, diplomats, and Congolese leaders were living with rumors, uncertainty, and even personal danger. Extraordinary security measures were in effect to protect them. The UNF provided guards for some embassies and diplomatic residences. Efforts to safeguard Congolese political leaders of all factions were not always successful. For example, Lumumba "escaped" from the U.N. protection and was eventually murdered. Early in 1961, seven pro-Lumumba politicians were "executed" by the Kalonji regime and fifteen anti-Lumumba politicians, including members of Parliament, were "executed" in Stanleyville. In response to an alleged plot against Mobutu, sixty persons were arrested on June 16, 1961. And so on, there were many similar instances.

Under these circumstances and with increasing criticism of his behavior, Dayal ceased to serve a useful purpose in the Congo. Hammarskjold respected Dayal and only with great reluctance did he give in to Congolese and other pressures to relieve him. On March 10, when Dayal was replaced by Mekki Abbas, a Sudanese, the new acting officer in charge was welcomed in Leopoldville by a brass band. A week later, Abbas informed Kasavubu and Bomboko that the Secretary-General had revised his nonrecognition policy and that he would now officially recognize and work with the civilian and military leaders appointed by the Central Government. The mood had changed toward greater cooperation between the U.N. officials and Leopoldville. But the deep distrust of the

U.N. military presence on the part of Congolese officials, especially Mobutu, which had developed during the Dayal period, persisted almost undiminished until the very end.

In the turbulent climate of the eleven-month political vacuum between September 1960 and August 1961, the conciliation efforts of United Nations officials were somewhat less frustrating than the efforts of the UNF to maintain order, discipline the ANC, end factional violence, and establish "freedom of movement in Katanga."

During this period, the size of the UNF fluctuated between 15,500 and 19,800 troops contributed by about twenty countries. The Force lost 5,000 men when Ghana, Guinea, Morocco, and the United Arab Republic withdrew their units because of Hammarskjold's refusal to support Lumumba and because of differences between the donor countries and the Kasavubu-Mobutu regime. It lost an additional 1,600 men when Indonesia and Sudan withdrew their units for other reasons. The slack was taken up by 5,700 troops from India, 1,700 from Nigeria, and 1,500 from Malaya. The first contingent of the Indian Brigade, which arrived in Leopoldville in U.S. Air Force planes on March 15, 1961, was not welcomed by Prime Minister Ileo who warned that "blood will flow" if Indian troops were to be deployed in the Congo. This negative reaction was based on the general mistrust of Indians in Black Africa, the unfortunate experience with Dayal, and the fear that Nehru and the Indian troops would side with Ghana and Guinea in supporting Stanleyville. This fear did not prove to be justified.

The large Indian troop contribution was important politically for the United Nations because Hammarskjold chafed under the Communist charge that the Congo operation was a tool of the Western "colonialists." Support from a leading neutralist government helped to blunt this attack. It also helped the Secretary-General to improve his relations with some African states. Prime Minister Nehru on December 12, 1960, had demanded the release of Lumumba, attacked a "new kind of Belgian imperialism," and said the United Nations was too passive. Nevertheless, Nehru rejected President Nasser's plea to withdraw his troops (then numbering 770) over the Lumumba affair. Nehru's reply as noted above, was to declare, in February 1961, his continued support of the operation and of Hammarskjold. He also persisted in his opposition to Moscow's troika proposal.

In a real sense India and the United States were the two countries the U.N. operation most depended upon, both for political support in New York and for military support in the Congo. Despite some differences in interpreting the mandate, the United States-India partnership remained solid throughout the Congo drama. The Congo operation would probably have collapsed if either New Delhi or Washington had withdrawn its support before the integration of Katanga in January 1963.

In addition to specific security measures such as taking over the airfields, guarding political leaders and diplomats, and making it possible for the Lovanium Parliament to meet without untoward incident, the UNF guarded U.N. and government installations, patrolled some troubled areas, took some modest steps to avoid serious fighting between the troops of Mobutu and Tshombe, tried to mitigate the bloody struggle in Katanga between Tshombe and the Baluba, and established "protected areas" for refugees.

Katanga Developments

Within Katanga, this period was characterized by almost continuous clashes between Tshombe's forces and the Baluba, and by occasional clashes of Katanga troops and ANC units from other provinces. Sparsely deployed and with an uncertain mandate, the UNF sought to prevent these skirmishes from erupting into civil war. Anticipating a growing need for a U.N. military presence in Katanga, a regional command was established in Elisabethville and gradually reinforced in spite of protests from Tshombe.

The tussle between Tshombe and the Baluba was for political control. The largest tribe in Katanga, the Baluba number almost 50 percent of the population and are located mainly in the north-central part of the province. In the Katanga Assembly elected in May 1960, Tshombe's Conakat party had had twenty-seven seats and the Balubakat party, a coalition of Baluba and other tribal groups, twenty-five seats. With this slim plurality Tshombe took full control of the Assembly. Jason Sendwe, the Balubakat leader, protested against what he regarded as Tshombe's high-handed tactics. The protest proved futile, so in July 1960, his party left the Assembly.

The endemic rivalry and mutual mistrust between the Baluba and Tshombe were exacerbated by the convulsions and factional strife following independence. But even before independence, Lumumba had attempted to gain Baluba support for his concept of a unitary state. Afterwards, Mobutu and Gizenga sought to enlist the Baluba in their respective causes. In general, Sendwe was allied with Leopoldville. He opposed Katangan secession and welcomed the UNF as a protector against the armed "pacification" efforts of Elisabethville. As early as July 28, 1960, Sendwe had urged that Belgian troops be replaced with U.N. troops. The lines of the struggle were drawn between two strong-willed men, both ironically products of the American Methodist mission in Katanga.[11]

In the many demonstrations, clashes, raids, and attacks which followed, numerous Baluba were killed. As of December 1960, for example, some 7,000 were reported to have died at the hands of the Katangan gendarmerie.[12] In this situation, the U.N. officials attempted to achieve political

[11] Sendwe and three aides were hacked to death with machete in or near Albertville by rebels in June 1964. *New York Times,* June 28, 1964.

[12] CRISP, *Congo: 1960,* Vol. II prepared by J .Gérard-Libois and Benoit Verhaegen (Les Dossiers du CRISP), p. 778. The authors quote Pierre Davister, the respected correspondent of *Pourquoi pas?* to the effect that one should not take African casualty figures at face value. "Generally one has to multiply them by two, by three, by ten, and still one does not know if the result approximates the truth."

conciliation within Katanga concurrently with UNF efforts to keep the peace. Conciliation efforts failed, but the UNF did succeed in somewhat reducing the violence and bloodshed.

In October 1960, the UNF assumed responsibility for order in the Baluba town of Manono and established two neutralized zones to prevent clashes on the edge of Baluba territory. At other places, UNF garrisons attempted with mixed results to suppress violence. Then, in January 1961, the UNF airlifted troops from Jadotville and Kolwezi to Manono to strengthen its position there. The situation had worsened. Showing little discrimination, the Baluba had attacked U.N. troops as well as Tshombe's forces. Swedish, Moroccan, Ethiopian, and Irish units were among those hit. On November 8, 1960, for instance, nine men of an eleven-man Irish patrol had been ambushed and killed.

In late January 1961, Tshombe began to import mercenaries to bolster his forces, and his planes dropped some homemade bombs on Manono and other northern towns. In early February, when Tshombe's forces were engaged in a major offensive directed toward Manono, the UNF attempted to prevent the slaughter of Baluba and the burning of their villages. The increased violence in Katanga prompted Dayal (who remained in the Congo until March 10) to urge Hammarskjold to seek a stronger mandate from the Security Council. The resulting February 21, 1961, resolution (giving force-if-necessary authority to the UNF) did not materially affect the situation in the first month or so, though a mercenary-led column moving largely unopposed toward Manono was halted temporarily by Tshombe two days after the adoption of the resolution, in accord with a promise he had made to U.N. officials. On March 30, however, Tshombe captured Manono with a force reported to include "Belgians, some Italians, and about 100 South Africans."[13]

On April 3, 1961, the first elements of the 4,700-man Indian Brigade arrived at the large UNF-held Kamina base in western Katanga. The Force seized the Elisabethville airport

---

[13] *Times* (London), April 1, 1961. Other sources suggest that the number of South Africans was smaller.

in the hope of using it to transport some Indian troops to the provincial capital. Tshombe called this arrival of Indians in Katanga an "act of war" and incited the population to attack U.N. troops. Thousands of Africans armed with knives, sticks, and stones rioted in Elisabethville and assaulted a Swedish unit which rejected Tshombe's order to surrender the airport. On April 5, some 600 Irish troops were flown in to consolidate the U.N. position at the airport. That same day, Hammarskjold told the General Assembly that he was strengthening the UNF in Katanga with Indian troops in an attempt to prevent civil war. He criticized Belgian advisers for serving in Katanga and condemned Tshombe for whipping up public passion against the UNF.

On April 8, 1961, Tshombe's troops attacked Kabalo in north Katanga. The Ethiopian unit located there fought back; it disarmed and captured a number of Katangan troops, including thirty South African and two Belgian mercenaries. This was the first time that the UNF invoked the force-if-necessary authority of the February 21 resolution. On April 20, Tshombe lifted the state of hostilities declared on April 3 against the UNF.

It is difficult to assess the effect of the UNF in Katanga during this period. Tshombe accused the United Nations of siding with the Baluba; the UNF did regard itself as a protector, especially of the civilian tribesmen. But U.N. troops were often the victims of Baluba violence. The whole struggle was complicated by the fact that other Congo leaders sought to exploit the Baluba for their own purposes. In early January 1961, for example, a pro-Lumumba faction of the ANC had seized Manono with the announced intention of establishing a separate state. The role of the peacekeeper is always hard, but in a situation of compounded confusion, it is even more difficult. It is probably correct to say that the UNF blunted the savagery, prevented some slaughter of the innocent, frustrated the designs of several politically motivated ANC units, and helped to deter what might have become a bloody civil war.

It became increasingly evident that the Kasavubu-Ileo-

Mobutu regime regarded Tshombe as its chief enemy and that the demand for the immediate withdrawal of all foreign military and political advisers in the February 21 resolution was aimed at Katanga. Hammarskjold persisted in his attempts to "eliminate the Belgian factor" in Katanga and elsewhere in the Congo, in order to dispose of one tangible and bothersome element from the complex legal and political picture. He recognized that Belgian technicians and advisers were needed in the Congo, but he and, more especially, Dayal were criticized for pressing too hard to have all Belgians in governmental advisory positions withdrawn. Dayal, for example, complained about the fourteen Belgian officers attached to General Mobutu's office and urged their withdrawal as quickly as possible. These officers were never compelled to leave because Mobutu refused to let them go.

Angered by Kasavubu's April 17, 1961, agreement with the Secretary-General calling for the withdrawal of all foreign advisers not engaged under his authority, Tshombe walked out of the Coquilhatville conference of Congo leaders on April 25. He was arrested by Mobutu's troops the following day as he was about to enter a plane for Elisabethville. Tshombe, who was held under house arrest, was subsequently denounced by Foreign Minister Bomboko for massacring Baluba. He was also accused of having incited rebellion against the Central Government with troops under foreign direction; illegal seizure of aircraft, arms, and money belonging to the Central Government; printing counterfeit money by issuing a separate Katanga currency; and of being instrumental in the murder of Lumumba and other political prisoners.

Hammarskjold vainly appealed for "fair treatment under due process of law" for Tshombe. At the same time, he was bitterly attacked by Kasavubu for overlooking the crimes of Lumumba.

On the promise that he would participate in the forthcoming July Parliament and support a united Congo, Tshombe was released by the Central Government on June 22, 1961. A week later in Elisabethville, however, he appeared to reverse his position: "We shall defend an independent Katanga and will do everything to maintain our nation in the face of all opposition." Katanga was the only province not represented in the July Parliament when Adoula was elected Prime Minister.

Tshombe's frequent changes of position can be explained in part by rapidly changing circumstances, different conceptions of what constituted a "united Congo," and conflicting pressures upon him. One of these pressures, for example, was his Minister of Interior, Godefroid Munongo, who on July 29, 1961, declared that Katanga "will not hesitate" to seek Soviet help if the United Nations and the free world "cannot or will not" find a solution to the Congo problem.

General Observations

1. The fundamental problem in the Congo—a fledgling government incapable of governing—was intensified in this period by a sharpening internal conflict which took the form of competing, provincially based, political factions, none of which had the power to impose its will on the entire country. This political struggle was further abetted by a factious and irresponsible Congolese army, and by external powers which sought to exploit the situation for their own purposes.

2. The authority of the United Nations operation, even after the February 21, 1961, resolution, was too limited for it to achieve the objectives identified in the various resolutions. Its means, legal and material, were insufficient for its ends. The United Nations was greatly constrained by its commitment to nonintervention which required the consent of the host state for any significant course of action, and Leopoldville was jealous of its "sovereign rights." As a result, the authority of the UNF was a great deal more circumscribed than that of a normal police force. The Force was neither the agent of a state nor could it act coercively, except in self-defense, without the

permission of a weak, vaccilating, and at times almost non-existent government.

3. The "force, if necessary," mandate was clearly limited to the prevention of "civil war," both in Hammarskjold's legal rationale and in the actual behavior of the Force. The larger mandate did, however, make a psychological difference, the full impact of which was not realized until the struggle with Katanga was intensified.

4. The fundamental role of the UNF continued to be unclear and controversial. In its external manifestation, the U.N. establishment in the Congo, both civilian and military, looked much like that of an occupying or colonial power. But it clearly lacked the authority of either. Armed with an internationally authorized mandate, however, Hammarskjold could —and occasionally did—ignore the wishes of the one political leader, Kasavubu, whom he regarded as legitimate. This occasional assertion of independent authority of the Secretary-General was restricted to matters of secondary consequence. In weightier matters, such as the retraining of the ANC, the right to arrest, or the right to search for illicit arms, Leopoldville gave the U.N. operation no authority and it did not claim such authority on its own. Hammarskjold continued to insist on his right to select troops and officers for the UNF and he resisted demands by Kasavubu to replace a Ghanaian unit and to recall Dayal. The Secretary-General could advise the Congolese, but he had neither the authority nor the disposition to command them.

5. The possibility of endowing the United Nations with authority to administer the Congo was discussed but never seriously considered. On February 20, 1961, for example, the Pakistan delegate, Said Hasan, recommended to the Security Council that the United Nations "administer" the Congo, governing and nourishing it as a trust territory until such time as "the Congolese people may be enabled to achieve their own political settlement."[14] Weeks before, Hammarskjold had told

---

[14] U.N. Security Council, Sixteenth Year, *Official Records*, 941st meeting, Doc. S/PV. 941 (February 20, 1961), p. 25.

the Council he "had no desire . . . to establish some kind of trusteeship in the Congo." An American appraisal from Leopoldville in June 1961 had found that the United Nations was dealing with a problem which in the past was solved by a trusteeship arrangement or some other form of external administration. Washington did not recommend the trusteeship solution, which was obviously incompatible with Congolese sovereignty. It may be interesting to note in passing, however, that control amounting to the imposition of external authority might have been legally undertaken by the United Nations under the enforcement provisions of Article 42, which are not bound by the principle of consent of the host state. Given the current international situation, the political likelihood of such a drastic step in 1960 was slight indeed.

6. Without invoking enforcement measures or taking over the administration of the Congo, it would have been legally possible for the Secretary-General to have negotiated with the Congo a status-of-forces agreement identifying specific rights and powers for the UNF that would have gone well beyond the actual July 29, 1960, agreement. The United Nations might have sought to gain temporary control over all military forces in the Congo. Such control would have given the UNF the authority to disarm or take over the command of the entire ANC or any of its units. A monopoly on the legal use of force is close to the heart of sovereignty itself, and perhaps there is a very thin line between having this monopoly and being the government. The right to disarm or command would have given the United Nations the authority to impose order and territorial integrity without necessarily violating constitutional processes. It would have virtually eliminated factional military force from the political struggle. An agreement among the Council powers to confer such authority upon a United Nations Force would have been impossible to achieve at the time, though in some future crisis in which big-power interests were marginal, such a drastic measure might be possible.

7. Little was done by Secretariat officials or the supporting

governments to clarify the relationship between political settlement and peacekeeping. The UNF was still embroiled in a highly unsettled political situation, having essentially only the authority needed to police a relatively calm situation such as the area patrolled by UNEF. The very term "peacekeeping" implies an existing cease-fire, truce, agreement, or political settlement to keep, maintain, or enforce. There was an agreement to expel Belgian military and paramilitary personnel, but there was no agreement on what should be done about conflicting factions in the Congo. The U.N. operation in its peacemaker role sought to achieve an agreement among internal factions and it made considerable progress. But it fell far short of achieving a united national government.

8. In the Congo peacekeeping effort, the Secretary-General continued to receive the support of a group of states led by the United States and was opposed by a smaller group led by the Soviet Union. India, by virtue of its heavy contribution of troops, became the chief partner along with the United States. Other states played important but smaller supporting roles. Notable were Canada, Sweden, Ireland, Nigeria, Ethiopia, and Tunisia. Britain continued to be ambivalent and France continued to oppose the UNF.

9. The relationship between the U.N. operation and the Belgian government during this period continued to be dominated by the single-minded devotion of Secretariat officials to the objective of expelling Belgian military and political advisers, particularly in Katanga. Preoccupation with this objective led to the occasional failure of U.N. officials, and particularly of Dayal, to discriminate between those Belgians who were prepared to play a constructive role in an independent Congo and to cooperate with the U.N. mandate, and those who were not so disposed. The Secretariat's position on the Belgian question frightened away, at least for a time, an undetermined number of Belgian specialists and thus had the unintended effect of denying the Congo desperately needed assistance in every sector of economic, civil, and military life.

This may have delayed recovery in some areas by years. Technicians recruited by the United Nations from other countries made a significant contribution, but in terms of quantity or quality they were not equal to the Belgians they replaced.

Given the strained relationship between the U.N. officials and Brussels, and particularly between Dayal and the Belgian ambassador in Leopoldville, there was little disposition on the part of the United Nations to explore ways to utilize Belgian technicians and advisers to help reestablish political and economic order in the Congo. The situation gradually improved with the return of Paul-Henri Spaak as Foreign Minister under the Spaak-Lefèvre government on May 10, 1961. This was a most significant event, not only for United Nations-Belgian relations, but for the future of the Congo itself. In the three following years, the earlier uncritical anti-Belgian bias gave way to a more realistic and constructive attitude.

10. Though the problem of financing the Congo mission became acute in New York during this period, it did not directly affect the field operation. The financial problem was a reflection of the deeper political division in the world.[15] The withdrawal of national contingents and the lack of adequate military equipment were more serious material handicaps to the UNF than the lack of money. After all, it was possible to spend now and pay later—as long as the United States was prepared to advance credit.

[15] The financial problem will be discussed briefly in Chapter 5.

3

The Katanga Problem

The issue in the Katanga is not self-determination. It is the threat of armed secession by a tribal area that happens to contain a disproportionate part of the wealth of the entire country. . . . The armed secession of Katanga plays into the hands of the Communists.
GEORGE W. BALL, DECEMBER 19, 1961

WHEN PARLIAMENT ENDORSED Cyrille Adoula as the new Prime Minister in August 1961, the Congo constitutional problem was solved as far as Mr. Hammarskjold was concerned. Writing to Adoula, he welcomed the new "constitutional government," and said that all United Nations aid "should be rendered exclusively to your Government." The U.N. Force, he added, "has only one goal, namely, to aid your Government in the maintenance of public order."[1]

The Secretary-General identified three specific tasks to achieve this general goal of public order. First, the Force had to help expel the foreign military and paramilitary personnel not connected with the U.N. operation; second, it had to prevent civil war, using force if necessary; and third, it had to protect the territorial integrity of the Congo. The dividing line between what the UNF could do on its own and what it could do only with the consent of the Central Government continued to be fuzzy. Hammarskjold was inclined to be cautious about exercising initiative.

In the eyes of the Adoula government there was one over-

[1] U.N. Security Council, Sixteenth Year, *Official Records,* Supplement for July, Aug., Sept., 1961, Doc. S/4923 (Aug. 13, 1961), p. 76.

riding objective: ending the secession of Katanga. There were many secondary problems, to be sure, but serious attention to them had to await the resolution of the most dangerous challenge to Leopoldville's sovereignty and pride.

The Katanga problem was also the chief preoccupation of the U.N. headquarters in Leopoldville during the first eighteen months of the new Central Government. Widespread consensus among U.N. members that the Congo should be united was reflected in Council and Assembly resolutions. There was virtually no support anywhere for an independent sovereign state of Katanga. No government at any time accorded diplomatic recognition to Tshombe's regime in Elisabethville.

Tshombe's insistence on juridical independence seems to have been largely a bargaining stratagem to achieve a loose Congolese federation which would permit Katanga sufficient autonomy to control its own revenue and to operate its own internal security establishment. Such a federation, Tshombe believed, would permit Katanga to continue as a prosperous mining state serving its white and African inhabitants and its European investors. He and his supporters probably would have been satisfied with the proposal adopted at the Tananarive Conference in March 1961. This called for a loose confederation in which each state would have autonomy on internal matters, but all would have a common foreign policy determined by a Council of State. The Tananarive plan (as noted in the previous chapter) was promptly rejected by the later Coquilhatville Conference and was, in any event, never widely supported outside the Congo. Critics of Katanga's secession policy opposed the Tananarive formula because they believed it would lead not to a national unity, but to the dismemberment of the country.

Hammarskjold and the new Adoula government both wanted to end Katanga's secession, but they were divided as to how this should be accomplished. Foreign governments which also favored Congolese unity were in even more serious disagreement in this respect. The Soviet Union, the militant African states, Leopoldville, and probably some second-level U.N.

civilian and military representatives in the Congo, all supported the use of military force, though they differed on the timing and the kind of force to be used. Given the sad state of the Congolese army, any forcible integration would have required the commitment of the UNF. Hammarskjold and his chief aides, the United States, other Western governments, India, and the moderate African states favored negotiation, persuasion, and other less-than-military means, at least until it became evident that these methods were not bearing fruit. Britain, France, and Belgium opposed the use of force to solve the Katanga problem or any other internal question.

This lack of consensus on the permissible means for achieving a common objective provided the backdrop for three armed clashes in Katanga between the UNF and Tshombe's forces. The first clash occurred in September 1961, and the second in December of the same year. The third round started in late December 1962, and had the effect of forcing Elisabethville to submit to the Central Government. During the uneasy truce separating Rounds Two and Three, there were long and barren negotiations between Tshombe and Adoula on ways to achieve a peaceful settlement of their differences. In these talks, in the Congo and in New York, the Secretary-General and his staff served as mediators. U.S. Ambassador Edmund A. Gullion, who replaced Mr. Timberlake in Leopoldville on September 6, 1961, was also active in these conciliation efforts.

The Mercenary Problem

Among most supporters of the U.N. effort, the undisputed first step for dealing with the Katanga problem was the expulsion of seconded Belgian officers and foreign mercenaries who were regarded as the backbone of the regime. It is difficult to prove that the Katanga government would have collapsed if these men had been withdrawn in mid-1961 because there were other significant components of Tshombe's strength, including Union Minière and other financial interests in Katanga, direct political support from Sir Roy Welensky (then Prime Minister of the Federation of Rhodesia and Nyasaland), and indirect political support from important sectors in Brussels, Paris, and London. The latter included some of the official representatives from these three capitals in Elisabethville.

Three distinct categories of men fell under the general and usually undifferentiated term "mercenaries." First, there were the 114 Belgian Army officers and 117 other ranks who were seconded to Katanga shortly after independence to build up and lead Tshombe's gendarmerie. These men remained until September 1961, and were then repatriated under an agreement between Prime Minister Spaak and Hammarskjold. The mercenaries recruited by Tshombe in late January 1961 to replace these Belgians comprised the latter two categories. By June, some three hundred had volunteered from Belgium, France, South Africa, and the Rhodesias[2] This number was probably slightly increased later in the year. A few of these men were given training and command assignments in the gendarmerie. They were the second category of mercenaries. The rest (the larger portion) were formed into an all-white "International Company" under the command of a Britisher, Captain Browne. Its strength was reported to be about 200 officers and men, most of whom came from South Africa.[3]

The objectives of the Katanga gendarmerie, which was actually an army of 8,000 to 10,000 men, were to "pacify" the Baluba in north Katanga, to defend Katanga's frontier against ANC attacks, and to guard against internal uprisings in south Katanga.[4] Mercenary officers and members of the International

---

[2] This figure for the first category, as of October 31, 1960, was reported by Rajeshwar Dayal in his Second Progress Report, *United Nations Review*, Vol. 7 (December 1960), p. 27. Information on the other two categories was given in the *Annual Report of the Secretary-General on the Work of the Organization, 16 June, 1961, to 15 June, 1962*, p. 3.

[3] CRISP, *Congo: 1961*, prepared by Benoit Verhaegen (Les Dossiers du CRISP, n.d.), p. 233.

[4] U.S. Army, *Area Handbook for the Republic of the Congo (Leopoldville)* (U.S. Government Printing Office, 1962), pp. 620 and 636.

Company varied widely in competence and political orientation. The most ideologically motivated mercenaries were French officers identified with the OAS (Organisation de l'Armée Secrète) who had fought in Algeria. Their leader, Commandant Faulques, was put in charge of Tshombe's paracommando school. These OAS types felt they had been betrayed by the French government and hoped that Katanga could be held as a bastion to defend the white political and economic interests south of the Congo against the black tide of African nationalism. The hundred-or-so mercenaries recruited in the Union of South Africa included misfits, drunks, deserters, fugitives from justice, and soldiers of fortune.[5]

More than five months had passed since the February 21 resolution had demanded the "immediate withdrawal" of the Belgian officers and the mercenaries. Making the expulsion of mercenaries the first order of business, the new Central Government put pressure upon the U.N. officer in charge, Dr. Sture C. Linner of Sweden, who had arrived in Leopoldville in May 1961 to provide material assistance in attaining this objective. An Indian battalion was sent to join the UNF Swedish and Irish battalions already in Elisabethville. On August 24, the Congolese government adopted Ordinance No. 70 calling for the expulsion of "all non-Congolese officers and mercenaries serving in the Katanga forces." Based upon the U.N. agreement of April 17, 1961, with Kasavubu, this decree explicitly excluded foreign advisers hired by the Central Government. U.N. officials held that the ordinance gave the United Nations "legal rights within the Congo" to implement the February resolution.[6] In Linner's view, this did not justify the expulsion of mercenaries by military force, though if force were used in self-defense while attempting to accomplish this, such coercion would be justifiable. He reserved the use of military force for self-defense and, as a last resort, to prevent or stop civil war.

[5] Interview with U.S. official, Pretoria, Republic of South Africa, Dec. 2, 1963. See also Conor Cruise O'Brien, *To Katanga and Back: A U.N. Case History* (Simon and Schuster, 1962), pp. 110-12, 124, and 197-202.

[6] U.N. Security Council, Sixteenth Year, *Official Records*, Supplement for July, Aug., Sept., 1961, Doc. S/4940 (September 14, 1961), p. 100.

Rumpunch: Prelude to Round One

The events culminating in Round One of the Katanga struggle (the eight-day clash in September 1961) are still hotly disputed; the explanations as to why U.N. officials did what they did are still more tangled and controversial and even less well understood than the actual events.[7]

"Operation Rumpunch," designed to apprehend and evacuate mercenaries in Katanga, began at five o'clock on the morning of August 28, 1961, and served as a prelude to Round One. By five o'clock that afternoon the operation directed by Brigadier K. A. S. Raja, the Indian UNF commander in Katanga, had arrested 338 men in Elisabethville and in north Katanga. Further arrests were then suspended by Conor Cruise O'Brien, the U.N. representative in Katanga, under pressure from the Belgian consul who promised to repatriate promptly all mercenaries: the 338 under arrest and the 104 who were still at large according to the U.N. list.[8] Precautionary measures taken to insure the success of Rumpunch—the occupation of the Elisabethville post office and radio station by the UNF and the guard around the villa of Katanga's Minister of Interior, Godefroid Munongo—were then withdrawn because Tshombe promised to announce over the radio that he was cooperating with the United Nations in the dismissal of all mercenaries. Tshombe was as good as his word.

The Belgian consul, however, did not fulfill his part of the bargain, explaining that he could only exercise legal authority over the Belgian regular officers; the other Belgian nationals he could merely advise to go home. The French and British consuls were in a similar predicament in regard to their nationals who had volunteered to serve Tshombe. Thus, by September 8,

[7] For fuller accounts and interpretations, see the official U.N. documents; A. L. Burns, Nina Heathcote, *Peace-Keeping by U.N. Forces: From Suez Through the Congo* (Praeger, 1963), pp. 100-31; King Gordon, *The United Nations in the Congo: A Quest for Peace* (Carnegie Endowment for International Peace, 1962), pp. 122-32; O'Brien, *op. cit.*, pp. 68-330.

[8] U.N. Security Council, Sixteenth Year, *Official Records*, Supplement for July, Aug., Sept., 1961, Doc. S/4940, Add. 1 (September 14, 1961), p. 106.

some 273 mercenaries were reported to have been sent home (some of whom later returned); another sixty-five awaited repatriation. Brigadier Raja and the other U.N. officials who had opposed the suspension of the Rumpunch operation felt even more frustrated when these commitments were not kept and a considerable number of mercenaries still remained at large in Katanga.

On the whole, supporters of the peacekeeping effort were pleased with the efficient and bloodless roundup of a large proportion of the mercenaries. Hammarskjold congratulated O'Brien. But, among Europeans in Katanga and their outside partisans, Rumpunch evoked a wave of hostility against the United Nations. Tshombe and his advisers were taken by surprise. He was now forced hastily to Africanize his gendarmerie. This angered the extremists, the so-called "ultras" and the OAS officers. His influential adviser, Munongo, was also unhappy. The U.N. command claimed to have evidence that the "ultras" were taking measures to nullify the effects of Rumpunch and to prevent any similar operation in the future. Tension ran high in Elisabethville and Leopoldville. Sir Roy Welensky stepped up his tangible support of Tshombe by placing troops at the border between Northern Rhodesia and Katanga. The anxiety-filled atmosphere was abetted by baseless rumors and lurid press reporting. Convinced that Munongo had hired a certain André Crémer to murder his deputy, Michel Tombelaine, O'Brien asked Tshombe to fire Munongo and later requested permission to arrest the Interior Minister, but Hammarskjold favored the arrest only if Munongo were caught in the act of inciting violence.[9] On September 11, after Tombelaine was arrested by Tshombe's *Sureté* (political police), the U.N. command demanded that all foreign officers of the *Sureté* leave Katanga within forty-eight hours. This time, Tshombe did not comply.

The conflict between Tshombe's regime and many Africans in Katanga was dramatized by the Baluba refugees who fled to

[9] O'Brien, *op. cit.*, pp. 232-44.

the United Nations for protection, shelter, and food. The number of Baluba in the U.N. camps in Elisabethville rose from 700 on August 31, 1961, to approximately 35,000 on September 12. This was a result of both the Katanga government's "pacification" policy in the north and the current unrest in Elisabethville. O'Brien warned Tshombe that his policy of "provoking inter-tribal hatred" might cause civil war and thus invite the military intervention of the UNF under the February 21 resolution.

There were anti-United Nations demonstrations, probably staged by the Tshombe government. The windows of the U.S. consulate were smashed, presumably because of American support for the United Nations. On September 9, Tshombe alleged that a U.N. plot was in the making to arrest him and Munongo, seize the Elisabethville radio, and disarm the Katanga gendarmerie. The plot, he said, had been planned by the United Nations at the request of the Central Government. Tshombe's charges were based on some fairly solid information. In an eleventh-hour bid for conciliation on September 12, U.N. officials sought to persuade Tshombe to expel the mercenaries and resolve his differences peaceably with Leopoldville. This effort failed. The same day, the U.N. company of 150 Irish troops sent to protect Europeans at Jadotville at the request of the consular corps was surrounded by a superior force of gendarmerie commanded by white officers. The Irish refused to surrender and on the following day were attacked twice from the air. The company was supplied with food and ammunition by UNF helicopters.

Morthor: Round One

In the meantime, back in Leopoldville, the Central Government had prepared warrants for the arrest of Tshombe, Munongo, and three other Katangan ministers. This was done with the knowledge if not the cooperation of U.N. authorities there. These five warrants were given to O'Brien on September

11, 1960, in Elisabethville by Vladimir Fabry, an American who served as the U.N. legal adviser in Leopoldville. They were presented in the presence of Mahmoud Khiary, a Tunisian who was chief of civilian operations in the Congo. The arrests, according to O'Brien, were to be made by the UNF as a part of "Operation Morthor," the latter being the Hindu word for "smash." Morthor, he said, also called for the UNF to apprehend mercenaries. The purpose was to:

> ". . . secure the post office and the radio studios and transmitters and to raid the offices of the Sureté and Ministry of Information and remove the files. Europeans and senior African personnel working in these departments were to be apprehended if possible. The flag of the Republic of the Congo should be run up at the earliest appropriate moment on public buildings and on U.N. buildings. . . . The Central Government would send down a Commissaire d'Etat to take over authority, in cooperation with Tshombe, if possible, in cooperation with the United Nations in any case."[10]

The final plans for Morthor were coordinated at a meeting of O'Brien's staff on the evening of September 12. At four o'clock the next morning, the operation was launched. Unlike Rumpunch, this new undertaking did not take Tshombe by surprise. It was not bloodless. Within twenty minutes, there was an exchange of fire in the vicinity of the post office. Later that morning, there was a coordinated attack against U.N. troops in widely scattered areas in Katanga. This was the beginning of an eight-day battle between the UNF and Tshombe's gendarmes in which eleven U.N. soldiers, about fifty gendarmes, and a handful of civilians were killed.

On this confused and fateful September 13, Hammarskjold arrived in Leopoldville on his last peacemaking mission.

In spite of O'Brien's many setbacks, in particular, his failure to capture his main prize, Munongo, he announced on September 13 to startled reporters in Elisabethville that the "secession of Katanga is ended." As it turned out, secession had by no

---

[10] O'Brien, op. cit., p. 249.

means ended. In legal, political, and military terms, Round One had become a great embarrassment to Hammarskjold, the U.N. Secretariat, and governments supporting the Congo operation. Morthor succeeded in capturing only one Katangan minister, Vice-President Jean-Baptiste Kibwe, who was released the following day. With the aid of the British consul, Tshombe escaped to Northern Rhodesia. The official party from the Central Government which flew to Elisabethville in a U.N. plane to take over Katanga returned to Leopoldville after spending several uncomfortable days in the Elisabethville airport under UNF protection. The Irish company at Jadotville was forced to surrender to Munongo himself. A lone Katangan Fouga Magister jet fighter plane, piloted by Europeans, dominated the skies. It carried out bombing and machine-gunning raids against the U.N. forces at Jadotville, Elisabethville, and Kamina.[11] At this time, the UNF had only transport aircraft. It immediately requested jet fighters from Ethiopia, but none arrived during the September fighting because of delays in Addis Ababa and the delay in obtaining refueling rights at Kampala, Uganda, then a British protectorate.

Tshombe's forces had machine guns, mortars, modern Mercedes armored cars, and Belgian standard NATO rifles. The Irish had 1940 makeshift armored cars and the Indians had antiquated rifles. In spite of inferior weapons and the lack of aircraft, the UNF, by virtue of the prior deployment of its units and some degree of surprise, did succeed in taking over some

[11] "During the fall of 1960, Tshombe began assembling a small air force, purchasing planes wherever he could. By the end of the year the Katanga Air Force included some 35 European pilots and mechanics operating 10 piston-engine planes, 5 helicopters and 3 Fouga Magisters—two-passenger jet trainers converted into fighter-bombers. One of the jets crashed and another was captured on the ground by United Nations forces. Seven additional commercial planes of the Air Katanga Line could be requisitioned when needed. Planes of the Katanga Air Force, operating singly, were used with telling effect against United Nations forces and they demoralized troops of the ANC during 1961, but their effectiveness was greatly reduced as the United Nations force brought in air support in late 1961." U.S. Army Area Handbook (Congo-Leopoldville), op. cit., pp. 636-37.

strategic points in Elisabethville as well as gendarmerie posts in Albertville, Manono, and Nyunzu. It also held onto the vital Kamina base.

Early on September 13, Tshombe asked the United Nations for a conditional cease-fire, but O'Brien did not accept the offer and shortly thereafter lost contact with Tshombe who had fled the country. Eventually arrangements were made for a conference between Tshombe and Hammarskjold to be held in Ndola, Northern Rhodesia, on September 17. On his way from Leopoldville to see Tshombe, Hammarskjold met his untimely death in an air crash just outside of Ndola. Vladimir Fabry died with him, and so did Heinz Wieschoff, deputy to the undersecretary for political affairs, and thirteen other U.N. personnel.[12] Tshombe and Khiary, who substituted for the late Secretary-General as chief negotiator, later signed a provisional cease-fire agreement which was subsequently ratified by U.N. Headquarters. Though Tshombe had come to the negotiating table acting like a victor, the resulting terms hardly justified this posture. The agreement provided for prisoner exchange; the return of the radio, post office, and other public buildings in Elisabethville held by the UNF; a joint commission of four members to supervise the agreement, including inspection of all military centers in Katanga; and an understanding that Katanga would be referred to as a "province" of the Congo.

Tshombe returned to Elisabethville as a hero. His Information Minister compared him to Jesus Christ, crucified and risen again, and he was hailed as "Tshombe the Magnanimous" for permitting the "defeated" UNF to remain in Katanga. His African gendarmerie commander, installed after Rumpunch, was hailed as "Muké the Victorious."[13]

---

[12] According to one theory, the Katangan Fouga may have been indirectly responsible for the crash. To avoid the Fouga, the U.N. plane crew had filed false flight plans and flew at night across the vast expanse of the Congo. Due to the shortage of U.N. airpower, the crew had been overworked and hence was accident prone. There are other theories of the crash, focusing on political motives, but they are not relevant to the present study.

[13] O'Brien, op. cit., p. 289.

The O'Brien Incident

By any measure Morthor had not succeeded. It had failed to end secession: its chief purpose according to O'Brien. It failed to achieve most of its specific objectives. Serious miscalculations had been made. With the first screaming headlines, many of which exaggerated and distorted what took place on September 13, Hammarskjold, who had just arrived in Leopoldville, was beseiged on all sides to explain what had happened. Why had the United Nations initiated military action? What was the legal basis for the U.N. attempt to end secession by force? Had O'Brien exceeded his orders, or was he in fact carrying them out? The British were particularly upset in light of Hammarskjold's repeated assurances that the force-if-necessary clause of the February Security Council resolution applied only to the prevention of civil war. They called for an immediate cease-fire. The French and Belgian governments were strongly critical. The Soviet Union, on the other hand, accused Hammarskjold of holding back after the initial success in order to appease the "colonialists." On September 16, the State Department expressed the hope that "hostilities will be brought to a speedy conclusion," but on the following day declared support for the U.N. effort to restore "the integrity of the Congolese nation."

O'Brien's explanation of Morthor was simple. The whole operation was designed to end secession. It was authorized by his superiors in Leopoldville, presumably with the full knowledge of Hammarskjold. Because of its political objective, the operation had to be more elaborate than Rumpunch which focused exclusively on apprehending mercenaries. Hence, the arrest of key Katangan ministers, the occupation of public buildings, and the seizure of gendarmerie installations became an essential part of Morthor. O'Brien insists that Khiary and Fabry arrived in Elisabethville on September 11 and that Khiary, as chief of civilian operations, had given O'Brien the instructions upon which Brigadier Raja and his staff based the plans for the operation. After the U.N. talks with Tshombe broke down the following day, Morthor was set for September 13.[14]

In legal terms O'Brien justified Morthor by invoking the February 21 resolution which permitted force to prevent civil war. Tshombe, he argued, provoked civil war within Katanga and invited civil war with the Central Government by secession. Hence, force would be justified to end secession because this would avoid both kinds of civil war. If one did not accept this argument, O'Brien had another one. Morthor, he said, sought peaceably to achieve a justifiable objective, the unity and "territorial integrity of the Congo," as called for in paragraphs two and three of the September 20, 1960, General Assembly resolution. In pursuing this objective, he insisted that the UNF had fired only in self-defense. This study has not determined which side fired the first shot on Wednesday the 13th, but it is clear that the sending of UNF troops to take over the post office and to apprehend cabinet ministers at four o'clock in the morning was hardly a use of force in self-defense. It is easy to see why such an operation would provoke shots from the Katanga gendarmerie.

Hammarskjold was obviously distressed with O'Brien's initiative: its timing, its announced political objective, the use of force associated with it, and possibly most of all with its poor execution. While never publicly revealing the extent to which he believed O'Brien was following or exceeding his orders, Hammarskjold's response gave the impression that he thought his Katanga representative had seriously misinterpreted, if not openly defied, instructions from Leopoldville and New York. Linner and UNF Commander General Sean McKeown denied they had ever instructed O'Brien, orally or in writing, to undertake an operation aimed at ending secession by the means actually employed or, in fact, by any other means. They disclaimed any knowledge of the instructions O'Brien claims to have received from Khiary. In New York, both Ralph Bunche

[14] O'Brien, *op. cit.*, p. 246.

and Brigadier Rikhye also denied any knowledge of such instructions. Ending secession by force would have been counter to everything Hammarskjold had said and done up to that time, though he doubtless would have had no objection to a second roundup of mercenaries supported by precautionary measures, similar to the successful August 28 operation.

Confronted by many serious criticisms of his actions, including the charge that the United Nations had launched a war, Hammarskjold acted quickly. He had to repair the damage to his reputation as a scrupulous observer of the legal constraints imposed by the Security Council mandates. In spite of this, however, he neither fired O'Brien for a breach of discipline nor even asked to see him.[15] In consultation with his top advisers in Leopoldville and New York, Hammarskjold issued a public statement on September 14, the relevant portion of which was summarized as follows in the *Annual Report of the Secretary-General:*

> At dawn of 13 September, the United Nations forces began once again to apprehend and evacuate foreign military and paramilitary personnel, for this purpose taking security precautions similar to those adopted on 28 August. At that juncture, the United Nations garage was set on fire, and troops proceeding to the garage to extinguish the blaze were fired on from the building in which the Belgian Consulate was located and from houses occupied by non-African residents in which a number of Belgian military personnel were known to be staying.[16]

This official explanation said nothing about ending secession, emphasized that Morthor was simply the continuation of Rumpunch, and portrayed the use of force by the United Nations as purely defensive. O'Brien says he knew nothing about any fire in a U.N. garage which he believes was a fabrication designed to appease the critics by obscuring the real purpose of Morthor —ending secession. The present study does not attempt to

---

[15] O'Brien resigned from U.N. service on Dec. 1, 1961, after he had been called to New York for consultations. He was never publicly reprimanded.

[16] *Annual Report of the Secretary-General on the Work of the Organization, 16 June, 1961, to 15 June, 1962,* U.N. Doc. A/5201, p. 4. (The identification of the full statement is U.N. Doc. S/4940, p. 103.)

establish conclusively the precise events of September 13 or to examine all the nuances of the O'Brien–Secretariat debate.[17]

Available evidence in this confused story points to a plausible explanation which emphasizes the mood and predisposition of O'Brien, Brigadier Raja, and their associates in Elisabethville. O'Brien was strongly opposed to Tshombe whom he regarded as an instrument of European interests. He was particularly bitter about the "ultras" who, in his eyes, prevented the more moderate Tshombe from coming to terms with Leopoldville. He was impatient, frustrated by the fruitless negotiations with Tshombe and what he regarded as the duplicity of the Belgian and British consuls. To him, the only effective answer to the situation was to end secession, by force, if necessary. Consequently, when he received permission from Linner (or Khiary) to resume the apprehension of mercenaries and was given warrants for the arrest of Katangan ministers by the U.N. legal adviser, he assumed he was authorized to end secession.

The whole problem of communication between Elisabethville and Leopoldville was further complicated by the rapprochement between Hammarskjold and the Adoula government. After all, Hammarskjold had offered to assist "exclusively" the new Central Government and held that Adoula's Ordinance No. 70, calling for the expulsion of foreign "officers and mercenaries" in Katanga, gave the United Nations the legal authority to expel such persons. The identification between the U.N. operation and Leopoldville had also been underlined by Linner on August 3, 1961, when he said that "if the Government used military force to impose its control on the entire national territory, and if resistance by local authorities led to bloodshed, the 'United Nations would not regard this as a civil war' and would do nothing to prevent it."[18] Presumably these remarks referred to Katanga. Given these authoritative statements by Hammarskjold and Linner, it was not difficult for lesser U.N. officials in the Congo to confuse a strongly expressed objective of the

---

[17] See, for example, the review (by Brian Urquhart) of O'Brien's book in *The Times Literary Supplement* (London), Nov. 16, 1962, pp. 865-66.

[18] Report by Henry Tanner, *New York Times*, Aug. 4, 1961, p. 6.

Central Government with a mandate of the United Nations, especially if the objective seemed to be in substantial harmony with the Council resolutions. Another cause for ambiguity was the fact that certain paragraphs of the various Council resolutions were not fully consistent with other paragraphs, and the Secretary-General had constantly to decide which paragraph should take precedence in any particular situation.

The open record does not reveal the extent to which Linner or his top aides cooperated with the Adoula government in planning the September 13 action, but clearly there was some joint planning. The government delegation, for example, was flown to Elisabethville that day in a U.N. plane, presumably with Linner's authority, and Fabry probably helped draft the arrest warrants. Under these circumstances, and given his strong desire to end secession, it is easy to see why O'Brien, and perhaps Khiary, may have misinterpreted somewhat the views and intentions of Linner and General McKeown. On the other hand, Linner himself may have been closer to O'Brien than the record indicates. As O'Brien ruefully says: "My instructions, taken as a whole, had the unmistakable meaning of ending secession."[19] Whether the breakdown of communication or understanding occurred between O'Brien and Khiary, between Khiary and Linner, or between Linner and Hammarskjold is less important than the fact that it happened, with the consequent setback to the U.N. peacekeeping effort in the Congo.

If this failure-of-communication thesis is accepted, the differences between Hammarskjold and his man in Elisabethville need not be explained in terms of insubordination or willful disobedience on O'Brien's part. Nor can Hammarskjold's official explanation of September 13 be dismissed simply as an effort to make O'Brien a sacrificial lamb for the fiasco.

The primary responsibility for what happened must be shared by Linner and O'Brien, and to a lesser extent their respective subordinates. If the failure of communication was between O'Brien and Linner, it could have been corrected at the last minute if O'Brien had submitted his detailed opera-

---

[19] O'Brien, *op. cit.*, p. 266.

tional plan for Linner's approval. Apparently O'Brien and Khiary, and perhaps Linner, were in too great a hurry to confirm and reconfirm plans because they wanted to get moving before Hammarskjold's imminent arrival. O'Brien frankly states that the Secretary-General would doubtless have suffered embarrassment "if fighting were actually going on in Katanga while he was in Leopoldville."[20] Why the great hurry? Was it to spare Hammarskjold embarrassment? Or was it because O'Brien or Linner feared Hammarskjold's veto? O'Brien's statement suggests that he expected fighting, but implies that the fighting would be completed by 3:00 p.m. on the 13th, the hour of Hammarskjold's scheduled arrival.

Khiary, as a messenger between Linner and O'Brien in this situation, was in a key position to facilitate clear communication. He was in an equally good position to "interpret" Linner's understanding of what should be done. When the full story is known, he may turn out to have played a crucial role.

The hectic atmosphere in Leopoldville and Elisabethville should not be forgotten. Events were unfolding rapidly. The technical problems of U.N. communication in the Congo were complicated by the operation's elaborate decision-making machinery. Legal and political ambiguity clouded every issue. Under these circumstances, the relationship of the arrest of Tshombe's ministers to the roundup of mercenaries, and the reasons for sending Adoula's official party to Elisabethville in a U.N. plane on the very day of the roundup were probably not critically examined.

The Uneasy Truce

The period between the provisional cease-fire of September 21, 1961, and the resumption of hostilities on December 5 was

---

[20] O'Brien, *op. cit.*, p. 251. Incidentally, if the military plan had been completed by the afternoon of September 12, a copy could have been taken back to Leopoldville by Khiary and Fabry. As they departed, Khiary said to O'Brien: "Above all, no half measures," see p. 246.

characterized by rising tensions between the United Nations officials and Tshombe, continuing disorder and lawlessness in Katanga and other areas of the Congo, resurgent separatism in Stanleyville, and greater efforts by the Spaak government in Belgium to eliminate mercenaries from Katanga. The two major political-legal developments were the cease-fire protocol, and a new Security Council resolution which extended the force-if-necessary authority to the apprehension of mercenaries.

On October 13, 1961, Tshombe agreed to a protocol with the U.N. command which provided for: (1) the exchange of all prisoners; (2) the creation of joint commissions with full freedom of movement to verify compliance with the agreement; (3) the withdrawal of U.N. troops from the post office and other positions in Elisabethville on condition that the provincial government would not engage in inflammatory propaganda against the United Nations; and (4) the use of airports in Katanga to the extent permitted before hostilities, but with the understanding that technical air control would remain in U.N. hands. The protocol also stipulated that all troops outside of Elisabethville would remain in their positions as of September 12, and that the United Nations would not consider the cease-fire to be violated if Katangan troops replied to fire from "some external attack," presumably meaning an attack from Central Government troops.

Prime Minister Adoula expressed apprehensions about the protocol before it was ratified by U.N. Headquarters on October 23. In reply, Acting Secretary-General Thant insisted that neither the cease-fire nor the protocol in any way affected the powers or authority of the Leopoldville government. Both were strictly limited to the relationship between the U.N. command and the armed forces of Katanga although it was signed in the name of "the Katanga Government."[21]

The exchange of prisoners did take place, though more than a month after the cease-fire, but other provisions of the protocol were not fully observed by Elisabethville. Radio Katanga en-

---

[21] U.N. Security Council, Sixteenth Year, *Official Records*, Supplement for Oct., Nov., Dec., 1961, Doc. S/4940, Add. 11, pp. 9-10.

gaged in violent propaganda attacks against the UNF. Some expelled mercenaries returned in civilian clothes and were given positions in the provincial government. The joint commission did not gain free access to Katangan military installations. Mercenary-operated Katangan aircraft bombarded Kasai-Katanga border areas and elsewhere in north Katanga. The U.N. command interpreted this action as a violation of the February 21 resolution which called for the "halting of all military operations" that might lead to civil war. At this time, according to the United Nations, there were still 237 mercenaries in Katanga. Previously 388 foreign personnel, including 317 Belgians, had been evacuated.[22] By the end of September, only a very few Belgian officers or advisers remained, thus virtually ending what Hammarskjold had called the "Belgian factor." In their places were soldiers of fortune from South Africa and elsewhere, and the fanatical "ultras" from Algeria, over whom Brussels had no control.

In retrospect, it may have been a mistake to have evacuated the Belgian regular officers so abruptly because their continued presence would have doubtless had a restraining and moderating influence on Tshombe, all the more because of Prime Minister Spaak's increasingly important role. Among those who believed this to be the case was Lieutenant Colonel Bjørn Egge of Norway, the intelligence officer of the UNF in Katanga at that time. In fact, Egge developed a plan for the gradual repatriation of Belgian officers as the United Nations provided replacements.[23] The Egge plan was rejected because it conflicted with the Security Council's demand for the "immediate" withdrawal of foreign military personnel, but it did acknowledge the fact that Belgian officers, who had respect for law and order, were preferable to the irresponsible mercenaries replacing them.

[22] Annual Report of the Secretary-General on the Work of the Organization, 16 June, 1961, to 15 June, 1962, U.N. Doc. A/5201, p. 6.

[23] Conversations with Lt. Col. Bjørn Egge in Oslo, Norway, Feb. 20, 1964, and in Washington, D.C., Sept. 8 and 10, 1964. See also O'Brien, op. cit., pp. 123-25.

With vivid memory of the consequences of having no military aircraft during the September round, the United Nations took corrective measures. The three Ethiopian jets intended for use at that time finally arrived on September 18.[24] By late October, the UNF had a complement of five jet fighters from Ethiopia, five from Sweden, and five Canberras from India.[25]

On the ground, UNF strength had been reduced by the withdrawal of the Tunisian contingent of 1,300 men (in response to the Bizerte crisis) and 600 Ghanaians, but both groups returned early in 1962. In December 1961, however, the UNF numbered 15,733 men, 6,000 of whom were deployed in Katanga. Tshombe had approximately 12,000 gendarmes and other forces.

Several untoward developments served as an ominous prelude to the November 1961 Security Council meetings on the Congo. The Baluba refugee problem continued to fester. There were approximately 35,000 Baluba in the large Elisabethville camp which was infiltrated by tribal thugs who attempted to control it by violence. Occasionally, Tshombe's police shot into the camp. The UNF took measures to protect the refugees and tried to persuade some of them to return to their homes.

A "police operation" by ANC troops under the command of Mobutu on the Kasai-Katanga border was thrown back by Katangan gendarmerie units backed by air support. The UNF did not get involved in this incident. Some Congolese soldiers in Luluabourg committed acts of brutality, and the UNF sought to protect the European population there. Most gruesome was the fate of thirteen Italian U.N. airmen in Kindu who were wantonly shot on November 14, cut to pieces, and eaten by mutinous Congolese soldiers of the 20th battalion in Stanleyville. On November 20, Tshombe accused the United

---

[24] *New York Times*, Sept. 21, 1961.

[25] As of November 28, the United States had airlifted 29,834 U.N. troops and 6,871 tons of cargo into the Congo; and 15,587 troops with 668 tons of cargo out of the country. This involved 1,263 sorties. The United States had sealifted 7,267 U.N. troops into the Congo and 5,992 troops out.

Nations of responsibility for the murder of the Italians.[26] To curb such atrocities the UNF planned to disarm the 2,000-man Kindu garrison, but later abandoned the plan as impractical because its unit at Kindu consisted of only 250 men. While undertaking to preserve order, U.N. officials continued unsuccessfully their attempt to reconcile the sharp political differences between Leopoldville and Tshombe.

After twelve days of heated debate, the Security Council passed a compromise resolution on November 24, 1961, reaffirming previous Council actions, deploring Katanga's secession and Tshombe's armed action against the UNF, and authorizing the UNF to use "requisite measures of force, if necessary" to apprehend and detain ("pending legal action and/or deportation") prohibited mercenaries and political advisers. The original resolutions of 1960 had restricted the use of force to self-defense; the February 21, 1961, resolution had extended the permissible use of force to the prevention of civil war; and the new resolution further extended this authority to the arrest of mercenaries. The resolution also authorized the Secretary-General to "take all necessary measures to prevent the entry or return" of mercenaries as well as "arms, equipment or any other material in support of such activities." The vote was 9 to 0, with France and the United Kingdom abstaining.

During the debate preceding the resolution, the United States urged that the UNF be given authority to destroy or otherwise render useless hostile aircraft and war materials "wherever necessary" to prevent their use against U.N. personnel or civilians. Washington also wanted the United Nations to be given the task of retraining the ANC and of mediating the political conflict in the Congo, and held that the resolution ought to take into account other secessionist challenges such as that in Stanleyville. Sir Patrick Dean of Britain opposed the

---

[26] King Gordon, *U.N. in the Congo, op. cit.*, p. 132. On July 4, 1964, Maj. Constantin Malongi, commander of the soldiers who killed the Italians, was sentenced to death in Leopoldville for sabotage, along with four other members of the leftist National Liberation Committee. *Washington Post and Times Herald*, July 5, 1964.

use of the UNF for dealing with internal political problems;
he warned that a United Nations-backed "military solution" to
the Congo problem would create a "very dangerous precedent"
under which the United Nations might find itself "at the beck
and call" of any state seeking to crush a dissident faction. The
Soviet Union supported the expulsion of mercenaries in
Katanga, but opposed giving the Secretary-General authority to
reorganize the ANC or to conduct negotiations to achieve
national unity. Secretary-General Thant promised to carry out
the new mandate with vigor, and added: "More determined
steps would have to be taken with regard to the training and
reorganization" of the ANC, and the United Nations would
"redouble its efforts to achieve national reconciliation by peaceful means."[27]

Tshombe's propaganda campaign against the U.N. presence
in Katanga was sharpened after the adoption of the November
24, 1961, resolution. The next day in a repeatedly broadcast
speech he said that "U Thant will launch a war on our territory.
. . . Not one road must remain passable, not one U.N. mercenary
must feel himself safe in any place whatever."[28] There were acts
of violence against U.N. personnel. On November 28, the U.N.
representative in Katanga, Brian Urquhart, and George Ivan
Smith, who later succeeded him, were seized and brutally
beaten by Katangan "para-commandos" and gendarmes while
on the way to attend a dinner for U.S. Senator Thomas J.
Dodd, an outspoken supporter of Tshombe. They were saved
from a worse fate by the quick and heroic action of Lewis
Hoffacker, the U.S. consul in Elisabethville, who physically
intervened and pulled them off the truck where they were being
held by their captors. Though Tshombe expressed regret over
the incident, his war of words continued.[29]

In this inflamed atmosphere, all efforts to discuss differences

---

[27] *Annual Report of the Secretary-General on the Work of the Organization,
16 June, 1961, to 15 June, 1962,* U.N. Doc. A/5201, p. 12.

[28] U.N. Security Council, Sixteenth Year, *Official Records,* Supplement for
Oct., Nov., Dec., 1961, Doc. S/4940, Add. 15 (Nov. 30, 1961), pp. 30-31.

[29] *United Nations Review,* Vol. 9 (January 1962), pp. 45-47.

between Tshombe and the United Nations and between Tshombe and Leopoldville failed. The discipline of the Katangan forces continued to deteriorate. More incidents followed. On December 2, gendarmes fired on UNF troops at the Elisabethville airport and set up two roadblocks in the town to impede U.N. communications. This was in direct violation of the protocol which prohibited troop movement "to reinforce a garrison or position." The next day, several Swedish medical personnel were abducted by the gendarmerie and a new barricade was set up on the road leading to the airport. Commanded by mercenaries and European "volunteers," the gendarmerie had virtually become an instrument of the "ultras." Tshombe was out of the country. There was mounting evidence that a coordinated attack against the UNF was about to be launched. Just before hostilities started, U.N. officials claim to have discovered a "battle plan," drawn up by Colonel Faulques, the mercenary leader, to "strangle" the UNF in the Elisabethville area.[30] India, which had more troops in Katanga than any other state, was becoming restless about the politically imposed restraints on the Force.[31]

Round Two: December 5-18, 1961

On December 5, the UNF undertook military action to defend its position in Elisabethville. Acting Secretary-General Thant authorized "all counter-action—ground and aerial—deemed necessary" to restore complete freedom of movement in the area. The State Department supported him. After an Indian unit removed the roadblock between the airport and U.N. headquarters, the Katangan forces opened fire with heavy mortars, machine guns, and rifles against UNF positions. This was the beginning of the second clash in which thirty-two

[30] *New York Times*, Dec. 22, 1961.
[31] See remarks of Krishna Menon in the Security Council debate, Nov. 17, 1961. U.N. Security Council, Sixteenth Year, *Official Records*, 976th Meeting, Doc. S/PV 976, pp. 36-37.

non-Congolese and an unknown number of Congolese were killed.[32]

On the night of December 5-6, the Katangans bombed the Elisabethville airfield. The next day, to prevent the arrival of Katangan reinforcements, the UNF took air action against bridges, railway lines, and the airfields at Jadotville and Kolwezi. From December 8 to 14, while the United Nations was flying in reinforcements, it reported military action at the following places:

> . . . at the Sabena Guest House, where the Katangese forces were cleared out on 8 December; at the airfield, where attacking Katangese forces were repulsed; in the neighborhood of the Baluba refugee camp which was repeatedly fired upon by the Katangese gendarmerie, with heavy loss of life; at the transmitter of Radio Katanga, which continued to broadcast calls to arms and which was damaged by United Nations jet aircraft; at Camp Massart, which was strafed on 10 December by United Nations aircraft; and at ONUC headquarters, which continued to be subjected to heavy fire. Elsewhere in Katanga, in particular at Manono, the gendarmerie was disarmed by the ONUC troops. On 9 December, ONUC carried out an air strike in the centre of Elisabethville, against the post office, which was being used for Katangese military communications and for inflammatory broadcasts. Other air sorties were made on 12 and 13 December against the Lido area on the edge of the town, from which the ONUC positions had been subjected to heavy Katangese mortar fire. However, ONUC carried out no bombing missions. While at one point a request for the supply of bombs had been made of the United Kingdom, the Acting Secretary-General subsequently withdrew it. ONUC's air and land activity was kept to the strict minimum; unfortunately, some civilian installations were accidentally hit, but there were only a few such cases. There were casualties among the civilian population, too, on these occasions, as also when the ONUC troops were obliged to respond to sniping from houses occupied by civilians. The Katanga forces consistently used the presence of civilians to shield their activities;

---

[32] On January 20, 1962, the United Nations announced that in the December fighting there were 21 U.N. soldiers killed and 84 wounded; 206 Katangan troops, including 6 non-Congolese, killed; 50 civilians killed and wounded. There were two substantiated cases of rape by U.N. soldiers. *Washington Post and Times Herald*, Jan. 21, 1962.

they placed their mortars near hospitals, schools, consulates and private houses. The frequent mortar fire in the centre of the town resulted in loss of life and material damage, for which the Katanga forces were responsible. In addition, these forces regularly abused the Red Cross symbol; Mr. Olivet, the chief delegate of the International Red Cross at Elisabethville, vainly attempted to prevent this, requesting Radio Katanga to broadcast hourly messages for that purpose. On the afternoon of 13 December, Mr. Olivet and two other Red Cross representatives were reported missing.

On 23 December the bodies of Mr. Olivet and his two Red Cross companions were found beside a burnt-out ambulance near the old airfield.[33]

On December 17, 1961, with the help of some twenty transport planes provided by the United States at the request of the Secretary-General, the UNF completed the reinforcement of its garrison at Elisabethville.[34] The UNF then undertook a three-day operation to establish a defense perimeter around Elisabethville. In this successful action, in which the United Nations was clearly predominant over Katangan forces, an Indian Gurkha unit cleared a zone on both sides of the road to the airport, Swedish units captured Camp Massart, and Irish troops took the tunnel under the railroad in Elisabethville. The Lido area and the road leading to the Rhodesian border were taken by Ethiopian troops, six of whom were killed during heavy fire from the Union Minière complex. In reply, the UNF struck buildings and other installations of the complex from the air with rockets and gunfire; it was later discovered that two Katangan military camps were located there.

On December 18, 1961, Thant ordered a temporary cease-fire in anticipation of imminent Tshombe-Adoula talks. On the same day, U.N. armored columns patrolled the streets of Elisa-

[33] *Annual Report of the Secretary-General on the Work of the Organization, 16 June, 1961, to 15 June, 1962*, U.N. Doc. A/5201, p. 15.

[34] Between December 6 and 21, 1961, U.S. Air Force planes transported a Swedish battalion, an Irish battalion, a Nigerian battalion, and Swedish armored cars from Leopoldville to Elisabethville. Approximately 100 flights were made, delivering 1,607 U.N. personnel, 901 tons of cargo, and 12 armored cars to Elisabethville and Kamina.

bethville to reestablish order. The UNF also helped to arrange for a train to take 382 European women and children to Northern Rhodesia.

Round Two was a striking contrast to Round One. If the September action had been a defeat for the UNF, the December operation was a military success. During the first phase the lines of communication broken by the Katangan roadblocks were quickly reestablished with minimum loss to the UNF. The strafing attacks by U.N. planes contributed to the success of the final operation designed to gain control of Elisabethville and the airport. Ironically, the strike against the post office on December 9 had produced no casualties, but caused an international controversy.

During the final offensive action in Round Two, undertaken after all reinforcements had arrived on December 14, the UNF captured Camp Massart, the main base of gendarmerie operations, and the Union Minière buildings. Katangan authorities fled Elisabethville.

The December operation at its peak involved 6,000 UNF troops, compared with 1,400 in September.[35] Some fifteen jet and other U.N. planes were used.[36] Offensive tactics were employed in the air and on the ground, and U.N. troops were *not* under orders to shoot only in self-defense. Brigadier Raja, UNF commander of the Katanga area, was given greater latitude in exercising military initiative than any former commander. This permitted him to employ offensive tactics and to move his troops into previously unoccupied positions.

Some fifty civilians were killed or wounded and, as far as can be ascertained, all those killed in Elisabethville, including several atrocity cases, were the responsibility of U.N. troops.[37] This was due in part to the fact that the UNF was taking a defended town from which civilians had not been evacuated.

The new U.N. initiative was bound to arouse criticism from

[35] *New York Times*, Dec. 24, 1961, Section IV.

[36] *New York Times*, Dec. 7, 1961.

[37] This is the judgment of representatives from several Western governments in Elisabethville.

supporters of the Tshombe regime. The removal of roadblocks and the air strikes of December 6, 1961, drew a strong official protest from Brussels and a barrage of criticism from the world press. On December 8, Foreign Minister Spaak declared that the U.N. "operations of war" had gone beyond self-defense; that the United Nations had used excessive force and had not always observed the Geneva Convention. In reply, Thant regretted civilian casualties but denied Spaak's charges, citing "the campaigns of violence, abduction of hostages, assault and battery, murders, the setting up of roadblocks, etc.," carried out by Tshombe's gendarmerie. He asserted that the UNF had shown "great self-restraint," and would have never used military action at all had not the roadblocks prevented "freedom of movement." Thant noted that "officials of Union Minière have proudly admitted the manufacture of gendarmerie armored cars and of bombs," and that the mining firm had made it "possible for mercenaries to go underground by putting them nominally on its payroll." He denied that the aim of the United Nations was "to force a political solution to the Katanga problem." On December 9, U.N. headquarters in Leopoldville announced that the restoration of order and the "arrest of foreign mercenaries" were the sole objectives of U.N. military action in Katanga.

The British government declared that the "U.N. forces are of course fully entitled to protect themselves," but they had no authority to "impose a political solution by force." On December 8, 1961, London agreed, with strong encouragement from Washington, to supply the UNF with twenty-four half-ton British bombs for British-built, Indian-operated Canberra bombers, provided that the bombs be used only in "preventive action against pirate aircraft on the ground." Three days later, however, under pressure from Sir Roy Welensky, a powerful section of the Conservative party, and business interests in London, the British government announced that it was disturbed by UNF "attacks on non-military objectives" and that it would not provide the bombs until the United Nations clarified its policy in Katanga and called for a cease-fire. The bombs were never sent. On December 18, British Foreign Secretary, Lord Home, said that the United Nations may "sow the seeds of its own destruction" if it neglected its first duty, "peacemaking and security," and turned to "the acceleration of independence and the eradication of colonialism, which is a subsidiary issue."[38]

The United States consistently supported the United Nations throughout this period. On December 8, Secretary of State Dean Rusk fully endorsed the U.N. action in Katanga, praised Adoula's "intelligence, moderation and nationwide stature," and said that if Katanga were not "peacefully integrated, the Congo will face civil war and anarchy, and be open to Communist penetration." Undersecretary of State George W. Ball followed this up on December 19 with: "The prompt action of the U.N., made possible partly by our diplomatic support, our military airlift, and our financial contribution, have kept direct Communist power out of the Congo."

At the NATO Council meeting in Paris on December 13, several foreign ministers were critical of American support of the United Nations action in Katanga. At the other end of the political spectrum, the Soviet Union accused Britain, France, Belgium, and other "colonial powers" of "openly sabotaging" the Security Council resolutions.

The Kitona Accord and the Long Stalemate

The military success of the UNF was reflected in the political settlement. In response to a message from Tshombe on December 15, 1961, expressing a desire to negotiate with Adoula, President Kennedy designated Ambassador Edmund A. Gullion to serve as his personal representative in the conciliation effort. Working closely with Belgian and U.N. officials, Gullion succeeded in getting Tshombe and Adoula together on December 20 at Kitona, the U.N. military base at the mouth of the

[38] *New York Times,* Dec. 19, 1961.

Congo.[39] Ralph J. Bunche represented the Secretary-General. About 2:30 the next morning, the two Congolese leaders issued an agreement in which Tshombe recognized the Fundamental Law, the "indissoluble unity" of the Congo, the authority of the Central Government over all parts of the Republic, and President Kasavubu as the Chief of State. He also agreed to Katangan participation in drafting the constitution, to return Katanga's representatives to Parliament, to place the Katanga gendarmerie under the Chief of State, and to respect the U.N. resolutions on the Congo.

As on previous occasions, the ink was barely dry on the agreement when Tshombe started to express reservations. The very day of the Kitona accord, safely back in Elisabethville, Tshombe said: "All the time during my negotiations with Adoula he was running to the Americans for guidance whenever anything awkward arose." The accord, he added, was imposed upon him and would not be valid until it was "ratified" by the Katanga Assembly. This was the first episode in a barren and abrasive dialogue between Elisabethville and Leopoldville that dragged on for a year.

Early in 1962, Adoula scored one political victory when Gizenga, head of the secessionist Stanleyville regime, was brought down with modest U.N. assistance, a development which had received strong U.S. encouragement. In the final showdown on January 14, the UNF, at the request of Leopoldville, provided token military support to General Victor Lundula, who defeated Stanleyville's 300-man gendarmerie and arrested Gizenga. U.N. assistance involved one Ethiopian platoon and consisted mainly of disarming Gizenga's gendarmerie, an operation in which not a single shot was fired. The following day, the Congolese Parliament censured Gizenga and removed him as Vice Prime Minister. On January 20, he was flown in a U.N. plane to Leopoldville, where he was subsequently placed under detention by Adoula. Though the UNF had no explicit authority to use force to end Gizenga's

[39] The Leopoldville regime resumed diplomatic relations with the Lefèvre-Spaak government on December 27, 1961.

secession, Thant said the action came under the "mandate to assist the Central Government in the maintenance of law and order and in the prevention of civil war."[40] Even if Gizenga did not represent a civil war threat, the U.N. police assistance provided could probably be justified legally under the general law and order mandate. Tshombe's stalling at the negotiation table was made possible in part by the fact that his regime continued to receive tax revenue and royalties from the industrial enterprises in Katanga. It is estimated that the revenue and indirect assistance from Union Minière alone amounted to some $100 million from July 1960 until secession was ended two and one-half years later.[41] Tshombe was also counting on a possible—or probable—withdrawal of the UNF because of the financial crisis then confronting the United Nations.

Politically, Tshombe benefited by the continuing division between the United States on the one hand, and Britain and France on the other: a division sharpened by the so-called Katanga lobby which carried on an active propaganda program in Brussels, London, New York, and Washington.

After Round Two, there was considerable debate within the U.S. government itself on the proper role of the UNF in Katanga. Senator Dodd publicly espoused Tshombe's cause. During the December fighting, an "American Committee for Aid to Katanga Freedom Fighters" was organized, listing some eighty well-known persons as members.[42] The committee declared that United Nations "action against Katanga," as well as United States "logistical support," was "illegal." On December 27, 1961, Assistant Secretary of State for African Affairs,

[40] Report by the officer in charge of ONUC (Opération des Nations Unies au Congo—United Nations Operation in the Congo), January 20, 1961, United Nations Review, Vol. 9 (February 1962), p. 27.

[41] Claire Sterling, "Can the Congo Go It Alone?" The Reporter, June 18, 1964, p. 29. See also, "Money Behind Tshombe," Observer (London), July 1, 1962.

[42] In January 1962, full-page advertisements of the American Committee for Aid to Katanga Freedom Fighters appeared in leading United States newspapers. Max Yergan, 79 Madison Avenue, New York City, was listed as chairman.

G. Mennen Williams, and Deputy Assistant Secretary of State for Public Affairs, Carl T. Rowan, denounced Katanga's propaganda campaign. Williams accused the "propaganda machine" of fabricating "horrendous tales of indiscriminate mayhem" committed by the UNF. Rowan said: "There has been a clever big-money campaign to convince Americans that they ought to support Katanga's secession" and accused Michel Struelens, former director of the tourist office of the Belgian Congo, of running the campaign from "plush quarters in New York." Four days later, Undersecretary of State George C. McGhee said that the Williams and Rowan speeches "were not cleared at the highest levels of the Department." The controversial Mr. Struelens provoked a drawn-out dispute between the State Department and several members of the internal security subcommittee of the Senate Committee on the Judiciary. Finally, in December 1962, he was ordered to leave the country or face deportation. "After a series of legal battles, he left voluntarily in August 1963."[43]

The futile efforts by the United Nations and the United States to get Tshombe and Adoula together on the basis of the Kitona accord were frustrating; at one point Thant even referred to Tshombe and his ministers as "a bunch of clowns."[44] On August 20, 1962, Thant promulgated what he termed a "Plan for National Reconciliation." Assuming that Katangan secession was the major obstacle to unity, the Plan called for the adoption of a federal constitution within thirty days, the sharing of tax revenues and mining royalties on a fifty-fifty basis between the Central Government and Katanga, unification of currency, integration of Katangan forces into the ANC in ninety days, the reorganization of a Central Government to represent all major factions (specifically including Tshombe's Conakat party), and a general amnesty for political prisoners. The Plan

[43] "Tshombe's Spokesman," New York Times, Aug. 3, 1964.
[44] Press conference, Helsinki, Finland, July 20, 1962. Reported in Congo Turmoil (Vol. 1, No. 2 of On Record, Keynote Publications, 1963), p. 38. Thant repeated the term "clowns" twice in this conference and added that Tshombe was "a very unstable man."

was based on proposals submitted by the United States to the Secretary-General on August 9.[45] Slightly modified by Thant, it provided for economic sanctions if the various provisions were not met within the specified time periods. Since it emphasized peaceful conciliation, it was endorsed by Belgium and, in fact, reflected a growing convergence of American and Belgian views on the desirability of salvaging Tshombe for a positive role in a unified Congo. Britain, the other NATO powers, and the states that had consistently backed the U.N. operation also supported the Plan, although Britain had reservations about the application of economic sanctions. The Soviet Union was in favor of the Plan without any reservation whatsoever.[46]

Adoula immediately accepted Thant's proposals as they stood, but Tshombe stipulated conditions. In the ensuing discussion between Elisabethville and Leopoldville, the basic terms of the Plan were substantially altered to meet Tshombe's demands. The cause of national reconciliation was not advanced and Adoula's position as Prime Minister grew weaker because of his failure to end Katangan secession. On November 28, 1962, he narrowly escaped parliamentary censure engineered by a temporary coalition of radical opposition deputies and representatives supporting Tshombe.

On December 10, Thant, after consultation with Washington, Brussels, London, and other interested governments, notified Tshombe that he had failed to carry out the provisions of the Plan, and that economic sanctions would be applied. The next day, Adoula asked seventeen governments to embargo imports of Katangan copper and cobalt: a request which was later approved by Thant. The Secretary-General appealed to Brussels to use all possible influence with Union Minière to withhold payment of taxes to Katanga until the problem of their

[45] New York Times, Aug. 21, 1962. For text of the Plan, see U.N. Security Council, Seventeenth Year, Official Records, Supplement for July, Aug., Sept., 1962, Doc. S/5053, Add. 11 (Aug. 20, 1962), p. 16-17.

[46] In August 1962, the Adoula government restored diplomatic ties with the Soviet Union which had been broken by Mobutu's military regime in September 1960.

division with Leopoldville could be settled. On December 19, 1962, one year to the day after the opening of the Kitona Conference, Tshombe declared that he would order a "scorched earth" policy rather than acquiesce to the forcible integration of Katanga into the Congo.

Concurrent Military Developments

During the year-long political stalemate that ended abruptly in December 1962, there were a number of military developments which, together with the political frustrations, pointed to the showdown between the UNF and Elisabethville. It became increasingly clear that the ANC was utterly incapable of dealing with Katangan secession. In spite of one modest step forward, efforts of the United Nations to retrain and reorganize the Congolese army had come to nothing. That positive step was the incorporation of the 13th ANC Infantry Battalion of 616 troops into the UNF in September 1962 in accordance with an agreement made the previous December. (The whole question of retraining the ANC will be dealt with in the next chapter.)

During 1962, there was a gradual strengthening of the UNF in the Congo and especially in Katanga. The Force grew from 15,669 men in January to 18,225 in December, of whom approximately 70 percent were deployed in Katanga and of whom most were combat troops. The Force level reached its final peak in March 1963, with a total of 19,782 men. The largest complement it had ever achieved had been in July 1961, with 19,828 men. The build-up during 1962 had apparently been planned in anticipation of Round Three, but it only came to fruition two months after the action ended.

The provocation and harassment of the UNF by Katangan gendarmes had a greater impact on the peacekeeping mission than the modest increase in U.N. military strength, the occasional clashes between ANC and Tshombe's troops in north Katanga, and the murder of twenty-two Belgian Catholic priests by rebel ANC troops at Kongolo. An important incident occurred on July 11, 1962, when Katanga celebrated its second year of "independence" with a parade of 2,000 troops in Elisabethville, despite an earlier pledge to U.N. officers that only a token "honor guard" would participate. In response, the UNF established a special checkpoint to control the route to the city. This led to a staged demonstration by several thousand Katangan women in which one woman and a young boy were killed.

One source of tension was eliminated on July 30, 1962, when the UNF completed the repatriation of 71,266 Baluba refugees from the Elisabethville camp, most of them to their tribal home areas. The big move was started on May 8.

The tempo of harassment picked up in August and September. On August 9, Elisabethville impounded, on the Rhodesian border, sixty railroad cars carrying supplies for the United Nations in Katanga. Other cars were subsequently denied entry, blocking food and fuel valued at more than one million dollars. On September 12, UNF and Katanga patrols clashed near Elisabethville and two gendarmes were killed. On September 20, a U.N. plane was shot down in Katanga by the ANC or by Tshombe's forces.[47] On September 24, two Gurkha U.N. soldiers were killed and several wounded by an unmarked mine laid by gendarmes near U.N. installations in Elisabethville. The laying of unmarked mine areas not only violated the truce, but was a serious violation of the Geneva Convention. This incident, for which General Muké disclaimed any responsibility, had a profound psychological effect upon Major General D. Prem Chand of India, the new commander in Katanga, and upon the entire Indian brigade.[48] Tension continued to mount in Elisabethville while discussions of the U

[47] A U.N. inquiry was unable to establish conclusively which side was responsible. See U.N. General Assembly, Eighteenth Session, *Official Records*, Supplement No. 1, Doc. A/5501 (*Annual Report of the Secretary-General on the Work of the Organization, 16 June, 1961, to 15 June, 1962*), p. 7.

[48] The writer and Lt. Col. Harold R. Aaron, of the Office of International Security Affairs, Department of Defense, were to be guests of Major Gen. Prem Chand on the evening of this unhappy event. The dinner was called off in mourning for the two Gurkhas. At the elaborate funeral the next day, all U.N. units, regardless of nationality, were represented.

Thant Plan dragged on. On October 9, the U.N. headquarters announced that Katanga was buying new military aircraft, constructing airstrips, and again employing mercenaries estimated at 300 to 500 men. By mid-December, Tshombe was reported to have "40,000 troops and gendarmerie, at least 400 mercenaries and at least 20 planes."[49] These figures were probably exaggerated.

In December 1962, Thant announced that economic sanctions would be applied against Tshombe. Lord Home again declared Britain's opposition to the use of "sanctions to impose a political solution." On December 11, however, Spaak said Tshombe was a "rebel" and declared that Belgium would support armed force by the United Nations or Leopoldville to end secession. Spaak's statement was an important landmark in Belgium's relations with the United Nations and Washington.

On December 20, the State Department announced the dispatch of an eight-man U.S. military mission to the Congo, headed by Lieutenant General Louis Truman, to determine in cooperation with U.N. officials "what additional forms of assistance the United States could provide to ensure the ability of the United Nations to maintain peace in the Congo." The mission was motivated in part by reports that the Soviet ambassador in Leopoldville might offer military aid to assist Adoula to overthrow Tshombe. The announcement of the Truman mission touched off a demonstration of some 100 Katangan students, African and European, against the American consulate in Elisabethville. The mission was also criticized by the Congo Parliament and the Soviet Union. In sharp contrast, the mission was warmly welcomed by Major General Prem Chand who was convinced that the visit promised not only increased American logistical assistance, but also signaled Washington's determination to support stronger UNF efforts to end secession if persuasion and negotiation failed. Prem Chand and Brigadier Reginald S. Noronha, the commander of the Indian Brigade, had earlier developed contingency plans for establishing free-

[49] *Observer* (London), Dec. 23, 1962.

dom of movement throughout Katanga, presumably with the approval of the Secretary-General. By this time, they were convinced that direct action was required.

Events leading up to the creation of the Truman mission bore out Prem Chand's interpretation of its significance. Late in the previous month, November, Ambassador Gullion had been called to Washington to participate in a fundamental reappraisal of U.S. policy toward the Congo: a reappraisal occasioned by the deteriorating position of the Adoula government in the face of the unresolved Katanga problem.[50] A broad spectrum of possible U.S. policies toward the Congo was examined, and the Truman mission was a direct outgrowth of this examination.

The arrival of the mission in the Congo, growing neutralist pressures for more forceful measures, Spaak's endorsement of military action against Katanga as a last resort, the disposition of the Indian officers to finish what in their view was the unfinished task of Rounds One and Two, the expected withdrawal of the large Indian brigade in early 1963 because of Red China's attack on India's northern border, and the financial plight of the United Nations—all these factors pointed toward one end, the final solution of the Katanga problem by force.

Round Three: Grandslam and the End of Secession

On Christmas eve, 1962, Katangan gendarmes started firing at a U.N. observation post in Elisabethville. General shooting followed, but UNF troops did not return fire. In a remarkable example of courage and restraint, Brigadier Noronha, without firing a shot, recovered a U.N. helicopter with its crew that had been shot down while investigating the firing. Katangan shooting continued and Tshombe admitted the fact. He promised to stop the firing, but by December 27 he appeared to have lost control of his gendarmerie.

[50] *Washington Post and Times Herald,* Nov. 28, 1962.

The next day, U.N. officials formally notified Tshombe that unless firing against its forces ceased, they would "take all necessary action in self-defense and to restore order." The firing continued, and on December 28, U.N. units started to move against gendarmerie strong points in Elisabethville.

Thus began Round Three, which the Indian officers referred to by the code word "Grandslam." It was started by Tshombe's troops. The UNF, at least at first, moved in self-defense and then only after being shot at for four days. The response of the UNF made it unnecessary for the U.S. government to consider further the possibility of direct military assistance to Leopold-ville.

Within three days, the UNF had completed phase one of its plan to establish freedom of movement in Katanga. Elisabeth-ville and the surrounding area to a depth of about fifteen miles was under U.N. control. The UNF also held the towns of Kamina and Kipushi and strategic rail points. U.N. fighter aircraft from December 28 to January 4 made 76 sorties and virtually annihilated the Katanga Air Force on the ground.[51] On the first day of U.N. fighting, Tshombe fled with his two most influential ministers, Munongo and Kibwe. At Salisbury, Southern Rhodesia, Tshombe threatened to launch an "Algerian type" offensive against the UNF.

There was a brief let-up in U.N. military action after phase one, presumably to negotiate with Tshombe; but on December 30, Robert A. K. Gardiner, the U.N. chief of operations in Leopoldville, made it clear that he was "not going to make the mistake of stopping short this time." This determination to move ahead was wholeheartedly shared by the U.N. command in Katanga and was in part responsible for a highly controversial incident that occurred between January 1 and 3, 1963. A UNF column, commanded by Brigadier Noronha, crossed the Lufira

[51] "No ONUC aircraft carried bombs and none operated over any city. . . . Seven ONUC fighter aircraft and one reconnaissance plane were hit." Of Katanga's "ten combat aircraft, all with the exception of one or two Harvards were destroyed, as well as all vital installations at the Kolwezi-Kengere base." Secretary-General's Annual Report, 1962-63, op. cit., p. 9.

River and entered Jadotville, ignoring an explicit order from the New York Headquarters to halt on the near side of the river. Jadotville was a major center of Union Minière, virtually a company town. Bunche was sent to the Congo to investigate this "serious breakdown in effective communication and coordination" between New York and Leopoldville.[52] He later concluded that "the machinery of prior clearance, coordination and reporting did not function well during the Jadotville operation," but that he "found nothing to suggest that the authority of the Secretary-General" had "ever been questioned by anyone in the Organization."[53]

As Bunche suggested, this celebrated case involved neither a technical breakdown in communication nor insubordination. It represented rather a justifiable exercise of initiative by a commander in the field confronted with an opportunity not known at headquarters. Proceeding with little resistance, the UNF column found that both the highway and rail bridges over the Lufira had been destroyed. Two companies, using debris, crossed and established an 800-yard bridgehead. Unaware of this fact, New York ordered a halt at the Lufira. The order arrived as U.N. troops were awkwardly straddling the river while under sporadic fire. To safeguard his position, Brigadier Noronha ordered the remainder of the column across the Lufira. They moved on into Jadotville, encountering little resistance en route, and were warmly welcomed by large African crowds.[54] The taking of Jadotville prevented Tshombe from making a stand there and continuing his resistance.

In his subsequent annual report, Thant says the premature launching of phase two was occasioned by the lack of resistance by Tshombe's troops and the on-the-spot decision "in accordance with good military practice, to exploit the situation and continue to advance." This decision, he adds, contributed to

[52] U.N. Press Release, SG/1406, Jan. 3, 1963.

[53] U.N Security Council, Eighteenth Year, *Official Records,* Supplement for Jan., Feb., Mar., 1963, Doc. S/5053, Add. 14 (Jan. 10, 1963), pp. 156 and 157.

[54] This brief reconstruction of the incident is based upon conversations with Maj. Gen. D. Prem Chand and Brig. R. S. Noronha in Chevy Chase, Md., April 19, 1963, and with American officials.

the "remarkable success" and "low cost" of the operation.[55]

Jadotville was also the scene of an unfortunate incident which was flashed to the entire world by the press, radio, and television, and which dramatized a persistent problem of the Congo operation—an inadequate public information program in the face of hostile propaganda. Two Belgian women in a civilian car were killed at a UNF checkpoint on the edge of the city when the driver suddenly accelerated the car rather than slowing it down or stopping it. The car was fired upon by Indian soldiers to the great embarrassment of all U.N. officials including the Secretary-General. Ironically, this tragic incident might have gone virtually unnoticed if the U.N. command had not invited the public press to observe the operations of Round Three. On the advice of U.S. officials, who had been distressed by the press distortions of U.N. behavior during the first two rounds, General Prem Chand not only invited reporters and photographers, but provided transportation and food for them. The two Belgian women killed in this incident accounted for about half of the European civilians who died in the entire 24-day operation.[56] There were some civilian casualties, again largely caused by the UNF.

After phase two, Thant temporarily suspended further military operations. A period of intense diplomatic activity in Elisabethville, Leopoldville, and New York followed. British and Belgian officials attempted to persuade Tshombe to give up his "scorched earth" threats and to permit freedom of movement for the United Nations in the remaining industrial centers. No U.N. or U.S. official was in direct contact with Tshombe at this time. On January 11, 1963, UNF troops entered Sakania, near the Rhodesian border. Ten days later, Tshombe agreed to the entry of U.N. forces into Kolwezi, to the removal of all mines and demolition charges, and to the surrender of all gendarmerie weapons to the UNF. On January 21, U.N. troops entered Kolwezi without resistance and were personally wel-

---

[55] *Annual Report of the Secretary-General on the Work of the Organization, 16 June, 1962, to 15 June, 1963,* U.N. Doc. A/5501, p. 7.

[56] U.N. casualties were 10 killed and 77 wounded. Katangan casualties "also appear to have been low." *Ibid.,* p. 11.

comed by Tshombe. This marked the end of the military phase of bringing Katanga under the control of the United Nations and the Central Government.

Throughout the operation, UNF troops encountered little serious resistance. The mercenaries, now largely French and South African, were much more disorganized than in the two previous rounds. Their French OAS commanders were unable to provide effective leadership. Tshombe's appeals for a "scorched earth" policy were largely ignored. During or shortly after Round Three, most of the remaining mercenaries left the country by way of Angola.

The Leopoldville government took immediate steps to reintegrate Katanga. Former Prime Minister Joseph Ileo was appointed Resident Minister in Katanga and went to Elisabethville on January 23. General Mobutu arrived the following day to supervise the integration of the gendarmerie into the ANC. The United Nations provided assistance to Leopoldville in the administrative and economic aspects of reintegrating Katanga.

On January 29, 1963, Thant said that the principal U.N. effort in the Congo would be shifted to economic assistance and that a substantially reduced Force would be retained to maintain order. India had already announced that its contingent of 5,000 men would be withdrawn by the end of March. Additional troops had been promised by Denmark, Ghana, and the Philippines. On February 6, Thant warned that a rapid withdrawal of UNF troops from Katanga might invite another secession attempt and that it would be necessary to maintain a military presence in the Congo for at least a year.

In a white book defending its activities in the Congo, published to counter the "misunderstanding and confusion" fostered by the "well-financed activities of the Katanga propaganda machinery," the Secretariat declared that force was used in Round Three in self-defense and "to establish complete freedom of movement."[57] The U.N. contention that great self-restraint was exercised by the Force is borne out by independ-

[57] *The United Nations and the Congo: Some Salient Facts* (United Nations, February 1963), p. 9. One hundred thousand copies of this nineteen-page booklet were printed in English and 25,000 in French.

ent evidence. Evidence also supports the white book claim: "By any customary standards of military appraisal . . . the casualties amongst both civilians and military have been remarkably light." Thant commented: "For a peace force, even a little fighting is too much, and only a few casualties are too many."[58]

Having strongly supported Round Three, materially and diplomatically, the U.S. government was pleased with the successful outcome. Incidentally, as a direct result of the Truman mission, U.S. Army trucks, armored personnel carriers, mine-clearing equipment, and transport and tanker aircraft began to arrive in early January. On January 17, 1963, Harlan Cleveland, Assistant Secretary of State for International Organization Affairs, said the U.N. military action in Katanga was justified, even though it was opposed "in varying degrees by several of the larger nations." Because of the Congo operation, he said: "There are no uninvited foreign troops, no Communist enclaves, no 'army of liberation,' no reason for a single American soldier to die there, no excuse for a Soviet soldier to live there."[59]

After heading a U.S. fact-finding mission to the Congo, Cleveland declared in Leopoldville on February 12 that the two major problems confronting the Congo were "catastrophic inflation" and the retraining and streamlining of the Congolese army. (The latter question will be considered in the next chapter, along with the role of the UNF during its final year and a half.)

General Observations

1. During the eighteen months covered in this chapter, Tshombe fell increasingly under the influence of the "ultras"

---

[58] U.N. Security Council, Eighteenth Year, *Official Records*, Supplement for Jan., Feb., Mar., 1963, Doc. S/5240 (February 4, 1963), p. 95.

[59] Address, January 17, 1963 (U.S. Department of State Press Release No. 34), p. 2.

represented by a small group of French OAS officers from Algeria. Ironically, the departure of the Belgian officers, who had a certain respect for law and civilian authority, virtually assured the triumph of the fanatics in the gendarmerie and in the government itself.[60] They left Katanga after Round One in accordance with Spaak's promise to the Secretary-General. Always sensitive to the actual balance of forces within Katanga, Tshombe became progressively less moderate and finally appeared to lose control altogether. When he began talking about launching Algerian-type guerrilla warfare and of a scorched earth policy, his faithful Union Minière supporters started to have sober second thoughts and showed some disposition to listen to Spaak, who urged Elisabethville to come to terms with Leopoldville along the lines of the Thant Plan. Whether Katanga could eventually have been integrated without sanctions is open to question since Round Three preempted the situation.

2. The ending of Katangan secession by coercion was the most controversial action of the UNF during its four years in the Congo. Critics of the operation regard the use of force in Katanga as its greatest mistake, while many supporters regard Round Three as its most significant accomplishment. In any event, the effectiveness of the use of force against Tshombe was determined partly by the UNF's military capability and the legal restraints of its mandate, and partly by the interplay of political pressures among interested governments.

3. In military terms, the three rounds were modest U.N. police actions, carried out with restraint in the face of considerable provocation. Though accurate casualty figures on the Katangan side are not available, it appears that fewer than 300 gendarmes were killed in the three operations. Probably fewer than 50 civilians were killed, including perhaps a dozen Europeans. Virtually all of these civilians were the victims of UNF military action. On the U.N. side, 42 soldiers and officers were killed and approximately 200 wounded. During the

[60] King Gordon, op. cit., pp. 138-41.

entire four-year operation throughout the Congo, 126 U.N. military personnel died in action. There were some atrocities committed on both sides. The Secretariat has been criticized by many supporters of the Congo effort for its reluctance to admit error and acknowledge atrocities committed by members of the UNF.

4. The UNF had inadequate skill, weapons, and manpower to achieve its objectives, particularly in the first and second rounds. The military setback suffered by the United Nations in Round One made this abundantly clear; hence, the effort to obtain fighter planes, trucks, and armored cars. Largely as a result of better weapons and more effective deployment, Round Two was a military success, but limited in its scope primarily because of political considerations. The slow UNF build-up continued through 1962 so that, by the middle of that year, the Force in Katanga was probably strong enough to have gained control of the province. Overly generous estimates of Tshombe's military strength, legal constraints on the Force, and the absence of adequate political support in the United States, Belgium, and elsewhere, precluded any U.N. initiative toward this end. Mr. Gardiner said in September 1962 that, if the United Nations had sufficient military force, it probably could achieve its objectives without using it.[61] Of course, this raises the question of how much is enough; but in any case, most supporters of the Congo effort agreed that the U.N. military presence was insufficient to accomplish its objectives at minimum cost, both in military and political terms.

The military inadequacy of the UNF was illustrated by two unhappy events which it was powerless to prevent. On January 1, 1962, twenty-two missionaries, mostly Belgians, were murdered by undisciplined Congolese troops at Kongolo in northern Katanga. Brussels accused the Secretary-General of neglecting the Kongolo area in order to concentrate more troops in Elisabethville. This, Thant acknowledged, but blamed the Europeans who supported Katangan secession, thereby

[61] Interview, Leopoldville, September 1962.

"jeopardizing the safety of their innocent compatriots elsewhere in the Congo."[62] The other dramatic example of U.N. military weakness was the failure of the Force to prevent the murder of thirteen Italian airmen by ANC troops at Kindu on November 14, 1961. To curb further atrocities of this sort, the U.N. command planned to disarm the 2,000-man Kindu garrison, but gave up the plan because its unit in Kindu was considered too weak to accomplish it.

Since the UNF had inadequate military weapons and manpower to hold its position in Katanga and to maintain law and order throughout the Congo, it decided that the establishment of freedom of movement in Katanga was a more important objective.

5. The military inadequacy of the UNF was not just quantitative. The U.N. command suffered because some of its units and officers were inferior. The Force also lacked an effective intelligence service; and the U.N. public information program in the Congo was almost nonexistent. There were, too, the unique—and yet inevitable—problems of control and discipline in a force voluntarily contributed by thirty-four different governments. Had it not been for the fact that Indians, Pakistanis, Canadians, Nigerians, Malayans, and others were accustomed to the British staff system, command and control would have been even more difficult. All three rounds in Katanga were commanded, and to a great extent manned, by Indians. Without the competent Indian officer corps under Major General Prem Chand and the large Indian contribution of troops, Round Three would have been virtually impossible.

6. The UNF never received explicit legal authority to end Katangan secession by force. With the adoption of the November 24, 1961, resolution, the UNF had the right to use force in self-defense, to prevent civil war, and to apprehend foreign mercenaries not employed by Leopoldville. The UNF was not authorized to use force to accomplish any of the other objec-

---

[62] *Annual Report of the Secretary-General on the Work of the Organization, 16 June, 1961, to 15 June, 1962,* U.N. Doc. A/5201, p. 19.

tives identified in the resolutions. With permissible means inadequate to its objectives and the murky dividing line between the authority of the U.N. command and the Congo Central Government, the Secretary-General based his legal case for the use of force on the right of self-defense and the right of "freedom of movement." Drawing upon the UNEF experience in the Middle East, Hammarskjold insisted from the beginning upon freedom of movement for the Force. This principle was written into his informal agreement with Leopoldville of July 29, 1960, and subsequent agreements; it became the chief legal basis for military action in Katanga.

In justifying the use of force in Round One, Hammarskjold rejected O'Brien's stated objective—ending secession—and his legal arguments. Instead, he explained, the UNF had encountered resistance to its legitimate operation of apprehending mercenaries and in self-defense was required to use force. In Round Two, force was used to eliminate roadblocks erected by the Katangan gendarmerie in order to establish freedom of movement for the UNF in the Elisabethville area. In Round Three, said Thant, the UNF could never have discharged its mandate to maintain law and order, prevent civil war, and eliminate mercenaries without freedom of movement. "It was with this in mind that freedom of movement" was provided for in the Plan of National Reconciliation.[63]

7. Though the United Nations is a political and diplomatic instrument rather than a strictly legal instrument, throughout its operation in Katanga the Secretary-General adhered closely to the legal principles of the Charter and the Congo resolutions. This was true in spite of the vagueness and contradictions within the mandate because Hammarskjold and Thant made a conscientious effort to observe the fundamental intent of the successive resolutions. Intent is a function of political purpose: in this case, the collective purpose of the supporting governments. This collective intent, which included constraints on the use of force and the prohibition against interference in the

[63] U.N. Security Council, Eighteenth Year, *Official Records,* Supplement for Jan., Feb., Mar., 1963, Doc. S/5240 (February 4, 1963), p. 94.

internal affairs of the Congo, underwent important modifica-
tions in response to changing conditions.

Britain, which all along opposed the use of force, still insists
that Round Three was a violation of the August 9, 1960,
resolution which says that U.N. troops "will not be a party to
or in any way intervene in or be used to influence the outcome
of any internal conflict, constitutional or otherwise." Considered
literally and in isolation from subsequent resolutions which
reflected changing political conditions, this categorical prohibition against interference in the Congo's affairs was violated
when force was employed to settle the constitutional problem
posed by Katangan secession. But Round Three cannot be
considered apart from other developments such as the November 24, 1961, resolution. This strongly deprecated "the secessionist activities" of Tshombe's regime; the Central Government's request to the United Nations to assist it to end
secession; and the increasing encouragement on the part of the
supporting governments for the U.N. operation to employ
economic sanctions or military coercion to resolve the problem.

While the U.N. operation inevitably had a profound impact
on the internal situation in the Congo, it would be incorrect
to conclude that U.N. officers were on the whole guilty of
illegal interference. In a series of interpretations, not challenged by the Security Council or the General Assembly, the
Secretary-General defined the policy of "non-intervention,"
under the peculiar circumstances of the Congo, as one designed
to secure a peaceful and constitutional solution to the new
state's chaos and division. It was only after all peaceful efforts
had failed to resolve the problem of Katanga's secession—the
most serious challenge to a united government representing all
factions—that the UNF as a last resort used force to establish
freedom of movement. So understood, Thant's claim that
Hammarskjold and he had "scrupulously avoided any support
for or opposition to any Congolese official or candidate, whether
in national or provincial governments," is true to the spirit of
nonintervention as interpreted by the unfolding legal and
political mandate of the Congo operation. Oscar Schachter,

director of the U.N.'s General Legal Division, has correctly observed:

> Can contradictory and highly general rules be administered by a non-partisan Secretariat? Obviously, there must be some exercise of judgment and discretion. But there is a difference between interpreting and applying these rules so as to serve a partisan or special interest or, on the other hand, administering them with integrity and fidelity to their intent and governing principles, irrespective of personal or political likes or dislikes. This is the difference between law and arbitrary action.[64]

8. Round Three did not become feasible until the U.S. government was prepared to support diplomatically and materially the exercise of military initiative by the UNF in Katanga. The Truman mission, which arrived in the Congo in December 1962, demonstrated that Washington had decided to strengthen the military capability of the UNF. New Delhi, whose troops would have to do the major job apparently had had no political or moral reservations against the use of force since Round One. The political change in Brussels was also a significant factor. When Spaak in a speech on December 11, 1962, called Tshombe a "rebel" and said his government would support the use of force, it became clear that there was ample political consensus in Europe, as well as in Asia and Africa, for the UNF to move. The Soviet Union had been clamoring for a forceful end to Katangan secession from the beginning.

9. The British position, which consistently opposed the use of force except in self-defense, failed to provide any guidance as to what the United Nations should do when its peaceful efforts to achieve a legitimate objective met with resistance.

---

[64] Lyman M. Tondel, Jr. (ed.), *The Legal Aspects of the United Nations Action in the Congo* (Oceana Publications, 1963), p. 86. Mr. Schachter's statement was made before Round Three, but it illustrates the effort on the part of the Secretariat to be impartial which characterized the entire Congo operation.

See also Ruth B. Russell, *United Nations Experience with Military Forces: Political and Legal Aspects* (Brookings Staff Paper, 1964), pp. 145-46; Burns and Heathcote, *op. cit.*, pp. 161-91; and Gordon, *op. cit.*, pp. 182-84.

The British view was based more on the fear of establishing a precedent for a U.N. "military solution" to internal political questions elsewhere in Africa, than on the fear of unfortunate consequences within the Congo.[65]

10. To a great extent the Congo operation was controlled by persons rather than by detailed procedures, rules, or laws. Given the vague Council and Assembly resolutions and the ad hoc character of internationally authorized peacekeeping missions, this heavy dependence upon persons in key positions within the Secretariat was inevitable. Lacking a codified body of procedure or even any substantial "common law," the Secretary-General had no choice but to exercise considerable initiative. This heavy dependence upon him and his chief aides has obvious pitfalls which both Hammarskjold and Thant sought diligently to avoid.

In this situation, the Secretary-General was subjected to powerful conflicting pressures, even to threats. The Soviet Union launched a scathing attack against Hammarskjold. While he successfully withstood this attack, it would be imprudent to assume that all members of the Secretariat under all circumstances would be as steadfastly loyal to the Charter and a mandate as he proved to be. The problem of confused loyalties or dual loyalties within the Secretariat or in a U.N. operation is a serious one. There is no way by which fidelity to the purposes of the Organization or of a particular mission can be established with certainty before a man is given an important post on the regular staff or in a co-opted capacity. While it is possible for a U.N. official to have ulterior motives, this study unearthed no serious problem of this nature. The problems of dual loyalties are, of course, present in all governments, but they are probably more likely to occur in an international organization which is required to recruit its staff from many states, some of which are in sharp conflict with one another.

---

[65] Interviews with British officials in London, Leopoldville, and Elisabethville, November-December, 1963. See also Burns and Heathcote, *op. cit.*, pp. 110-11 and 124-25.

The fact that the Congo operation remained as loyal as it did to the Council resolutions was due in part to the impartiality of the Secretary-General and in part to fortuitous or planned circumstances. Three of Hammarskjold's chief aides were American. The Congo story would doubtless have turned out differently had they been Russian, French, or even British. In addition to consulting the Council, the Assembly, and the Congo Advisory Committee, the Secretary-General sought the advice of an informal intimate group sometimes referred to as the "Congo Club," which included three Americans, two Indians, one Briton, and one Ghanaian.[66] This group obviously had considerable influence in determining the direction of the Congo effort.

The Secretary-General also consulted directly with interested governments, the most influential of which was the United States, without whose diplomatic, financial, and logistical support the operation would have faltered and probably collapsed. The State Department presented its views in New York, Leopoldville, and Elisabethville. The American ambassador in the Congo was in constant touch with both U.N. and Congo officials. The U.S. consul in Katanga made himself available to U.N. civilian and military officers. The American military attache was in close touch with U.N. headquarters in Leopoldville.

In New York, the U.S. permanent representative to the United Nations met frequently with the Secretary-General. Other members of the U.S. Mission to the United Nations saw Undersecretary Bunche and other U.N. officials almost daily. The military officers on the staff of the Mission performed a

[66] An article in the New York Times on October 19, 1961, identified the members of the Congo Club as follows: "Andrew W. Cordier (U.S.), Under-Secretary of General Assembly Affairs; Ralph J. Bunche (U.S.), Under-Secretary for Special Political Affairs; C. V. Narasimhan (India), Staff Aide to Hammarskjold; Brigadier I. J. Rikhye (India), Military Advisor to the Secretary-General; Sir Alexander MacFarquhar (U.K.), Special Adviser on Civilian Operations in the Congo; and Robert W. Gardiner of Ghana, an economic- and social-affairs officer." Heinz Wieschhoff (U.S.), Bunche's deputy, also belonged to the "Congo Club."

liaison function between the office of the Secretary-General's military adviser and the Department of Defense in Washington. In processing U.N. requests for logistical support and supplies transmitted from Leopoldville to New York, and in other matters requiring policy determination by Washington, these military officers worked closely with their political counterparts in the Mission and the State Department.

These continuing and multiple contacts with a powerful government that supported the operation had a profound and inescapable impact upon the direction and quality of the total Congo effort. This fact can be welcomed or deplored, depending upon the perspective of the viewer. It should be clear, however, that Washington was only one of many governments whose views were vigorously brought to the attention of the Secretariat. Britain, France, the Soviet Union, smaller Western states, and neutralist states also presented their positions in terms of their interests. The Secretary-General attempted to take into account all criticisms and suggestions as he sought to fulfill the mandate.

The United States may seem to have been more influential than it really was because the American interest in stability in the Congo and a constitutional solution to the internal conflict there corresponded to a remarkable degree with the central objectives of the U.N. effort. Seen in this light, the Soviet charge that the Secretary-General was a puppet of the State Department is absurd.

4

The Congo Army and
Internal Security

*A reorganized and disciplined Congolese National
Army is a most, perhaps the most, vital problem.*
RALPH J. BUNCHE, AUGUST 21, 1960

IT IS CUSTOMARY for diplomats to be more optimistic
in public than they are in private. This was certainly true
of official appraisals of the Congo situation made immediately
after the end of Katangan secession. Pleased by the outcome
of Round Three, Secretary-General Thant concluded that the
mandate to protect the "territorial integrity and political independence" of the Congo, to prevent civil war, and to remove
foreign mercenaries had been largely fulfilled except for an
alert "caretaker role." As for the maintenance of law and order,
he acknowledged that there was "much still to be done."[1] The
U.N. white book said "the military phase" had ended, and the
"national government exercising effective authority" was a "vast
improvement over the chaotic situation" of July 1960. It also
acknowledged that "the state of law and order" left something
to be desired and that the ANC needed "continuing assistance
from the United Nations Force" to maintain "internal security."[2]

[1] U.N. Security Council, Eighteenth Year, *Official Records*, Supplement for
Jan., Feb., Mar., 1963, Doc. S/5240 (February 4, 1963), pp. 98 and 99.
[2] *The United Nations and the Congo: Some Salient Facts* (United Nations,
February 1963), pp. 14-17.

122

Before secession was fully ended, Harlan Cleveland said the Congo was "about to be free and whole again" and was "moving towards law and order."[3] As a result of U.N. intervention, said another U.S. official, "reasonable quiet has returned to the Congo" and the United Nations had helped "to maintain a free, moderate government," to deter the "dangers of civil war," and to "avoid direct Great Power intervention." Further, "secession from the left and from the right," has been ended and the "ambitions of the Communists to establish a base in the heart of Central Africa," have been spiked.[4]

Events in 1963 and the three armed revolts in the first half of 1964 proved these statements to be too optimistic. But they were, of course, public utterances that were qualified by private reservations. United Nations and State Department officials knew that great problems remained in the security field—the continued lawlessness and indiscipline of Congolese troops, tribal feuding, and bitter political conflict. Although there was a recognized Central Government, it was still weak, inexperienced, rent by factions, and demoralized by incompetence and corruption. These political problems were exacerbated by a desperate economic situation—inflation, fiscal irresponsibility, unemployment, and an unfavorable environment for international investment. The continued chaos and confusion of the Congo invited covert Communist penetration. The Congo was still a state in search of a nation.

The Irresponsibility of the Congo Army

The mutiny of the ANC was the proximate cause of the Congo crisis in 1960. Since then, its indiscipline, lawlessness, and factionalism have been major factors in the continuing

[3] Address, January 17, 1963 (U.S. Department of State Press Release 34), p. 2.

[4] Joseph Sisco, Director, Office of U.N. Political Affairs, Department of State, Address, March 11, 1963 (U.S. Department of State Press Release 120), pp. 4 and 5.

turbulence. The ANC has never been a united national army. Only a portion of the Congolese soldiers have ever been under the effective control of the Central Government. Hence, the instrument designed to maintain order has in fact been a cause of disorder. Incidents of indiscipline range all the way from extortion, wanton murder, and rape, to attacks on UNF units, mutiny, and the arrest and attempted assassination of the ANC's Commander in Chief, Mobutu. In a four-month period, from May through August 1963, one unpublished U.S. tabulation (admittedly incomplete) of events "traceable to the instability of Congolese security forces" lists 60 unlawful incidents, not including "ordinary" crimes. Secretary-General Thant summarized the situation with diplomatic understatement in his final report on the Congo operation:

> . . . the ANC is still insufficiently trained and officered to cope with any major crisis. Most of the Congolese troops still show, in emergency situations, inadequate discipline and devotion to duty or country. Good officers, who are competent and earnest, would seem to be the exception rather than the rule. The result is that there is little authority at the top and little soldierly spirit in the ranks. The lack of adequate leadership and of an organic chain of command is perhaps the main cause for the present ineffectiveness of the ANC. The lack of logistical organization and sound staff work is also a major obstacle to more effective operation.[5]

In the same report, Thant notes that the "maintenance of law and order has been, since July 1960, the crucial problem of the Congo" and that U.N. responsibility in this area "was linked with its task of assisting the Government in reorganizing and training the Congolese security forces." In this task, he adds, the United Nations has "encountered great difficulties."[6] The Security Council mandate to substitute for and simultaneously to reorganize the ANC was explicit in the first informal request for U.N. assistance from Lumumba transmitted by Dr. Bunche to New York on July 11, 1960; but the indiscipline of the ANC was not mentioned in the Central Government's formal written

[5] U.N. Security Council, "Report by the Secretary-General on the Withdrawal of the United Nations in the Congo and on Other Aspects of the United Nations Operation There," Doc. S/5784 (mimeographed June 29, 1964), p. 30.
[6] Ibid., p. 29.

request on the following day which focused on Belgian "aggression." No Council resolution ever specifically authorized the United Nations to reorganize or retrain the ANC, but the Congo Advisory Committee, the Secretariat, the United States, and other supporting states assumed that the U.N. mission should assist the Congolese government to do precisely this. The first Council resolution spoke of assistance until the "national security forces may be able, in the opinion of the Government, to meet fully their tasks." The February 21, 1961, resolution said ANC units "should be reorganized and brought under discipline and control" so they would not interfere in "the political life of the Congo;" but it did not indicate what role the United Nations should play.

U.N. Failure To Retrain the ANC

Even though General Alexander did not succeed in persuading the U.N. command to disarm the ANC, which he regarded as a necessary first step toward reorganization, a U.N. program of training Congolese troops was begun in August 1960. This was before the Mobutu coup when General Hammou Kettani of Morocco was the deputy UNF commander; but the training program was brought to an abrupt halt by the political breakdown the following month. A year later, in October, at the request of the Central Government, preparations were made by Major General Iyassu Mengesha of Ethiopia for a United Nations-operated ANC officer school at Kamina; but General Mobutu never sent any cadets for training. These failures made it clear that the United Nations was getting nowhere in retraining the ANC. One of the reasons was Mobutu's preference for bilateral assistance, particularly training officers from Belgium. He had maintained a small group of Belgian advisers all along in the Defense Ministry and was anxious to enlarge the number of advisers from Brussels. On the wall of his office hung the pictures of all but one of the past commanders of the Belgian *Force publique;* the exception was the last, blunt General Janssens. When Mobutu was asked why the pictures were there, he replied that even though there was political discontinuity in the Congo, there should be military continuity.[7]

Incidental training may have been provided for some six to eight hundred Congolese when the 13th ANC Battalion was attached to the UNF from September 1962 until it withdrew in February 1964.

In sum, the United Nations made virtually no provision for the maintenance of internal security in the period following the departure of its troops. According to many supporters of the effort, this was its greatest failure. That the ANC was, for all practical purposes, as ill-disciplined and irresponsible in 1964 as it was in 1960 is generally accepted as a fact. But there is disagreement as to where the fault lies. U.N. officials place most of the blame on the Congolese government. Many disinterested observers, including U.S. diplomatic and military officials, believe that the United Nations was also at fault. Obviously the failure to discipline the ANC was rooted in a combination of interrelated causes. Three are especially important.

1. The resolutions did not give the UNF authority to disarm or train Congolese troops without the consent of the Central government. To have done so against the will of the Congolese government would have been a serious infringement of sovereignty:

2. The Central Government did not cooperate with U.N. training plans, in part because of continuing mutual distrust between some Congolese officials, particularly Mobutu, and some U.N. officials. This distrust was generated in the Dayal period, as noted in Chapter 2, and persisted until the UNF left in 1964. The relations between Mobutu and General Rikhye, the Secretary-General's military adviser, were also strained. This was also generally true of the relationship between Mobutu and the U.N. Force commanders and liaison officers. One Western official who observed the situation closely for years in Leopoldville said that "at no time did the United Nations desist in re-

[7] Interview, Leopoldville, September 1962.

garding the Congo as an enemy state from a military point of view. . . . I do feel that more intensive and sincere efforts to cooperate on the part of senior U.N. Military Commanders could have resulted in Mobutu's being more forthcoming and cooperative."[8] Such as assessment may be an exaggeration, but its general tone is in line with the comments of other observers.

3. The Secretary-General did not place as high a priority upon the retraining objective as he did on the settlement of the Katanga question. In spite of a lack of explicit authority, many observers believe he should have worked harder and more consistently to achieve a working agreement with the Central Government on training the ANC which both Hammarskjold and Thant said was a central, if not the central, problem in the Congo. Within the constraints of consent, some things could have been done which were not done, including a diligent effort to send U.N. representatives to Leopoldville who could have worked more effectively with Congolese authorities in this sensitive area. The reluctance of Hammarskjold to replace Dayal, for example, did not help the situation. Given the Congolese antipathy toward Indians, the temporary replacement of Dayal with General Rikhye, another Indian, was unwise. Further, as noted in Chapter 1, in the early weeks of chaos when the disarmament of mutinous ANC units was a possibility, the United Nations had no plan to move ahead. Since the Secretary-General authorized the U.N. takeover of the airports and the Leopoldville radio station against Lumumba's will, he might have authorized the UNF to disarm irresponsible Congolese soldiers without Lumumba's consent.

Perhaps the United Nations did the best it could under the extenuating circumstances, but these after-the-fact observations may suggest some guidelines for the future.

The Greene Plan and Bilateral Assistance

Anticipating the inevitable withdrawal of the UNF from the Congo and recognizing that the ANC would not accept direct

[8] Letter to the author, October 1, 1964.

U.N. assistance, Washington in July 1962 sent a military advisory team to the Congo to appraise the situation. The Greene Plan, named after Colonel Michael J. L. Greene, USA, who led the team, eventually emerged as a result of this appraisal. The purpose of the Plan was to assist the Congo to modernize and train the ANC and provincial gendarmerie through a series of bilateral assistance programs channeled through and coordinated by the United Nations in accordance with the Council resolutions. After considerable debate within the U.S. government, discussion in Leopoldville, and confidential consultation with U.N. officials, the United States approached five governments interested in assisting the Congo: Belgium, Canada, Israel, Italy, and Norway. Privately, Thant encouraged the Greene Plan and on February 4, 1963, he said it had become "advisable and desirable" to increase "bilateral aid."[9]

On February 26, 1963, Adoula's office informed Robert A. K. Gardiner, the U.N. officer in charge in Leopoldville, that his government had decided to request the following states "for assistance in modernizing the ANC: 1. Canada, for technical schools (communications); 2. Italy for the Air Force; 3. Norway, for the Navy; 4. Israel, for the training of paratroopers; 5. Belgium, for technicians for ANC Headquarters and the various units. Belgium will also assist us in the matter of our bases, the Gendarmerie, and our various military schools." The letter added that the United States "will do no more than provide the equipment necessary to ensure the success of these technical assistance measures."[10]

This was a controversial communication because it introduced the prospect of direct military assistance which ran counter to Hammarskjold's original rule against external aid to the Congo not channeled through the United Nations. The

[9] U.N. Security Council, Eighteenth Year, *Official Records*, Supplement for Jan., Feb., March, 1963, Doc. S/5240 (February 4, 1963), p. 101.

[10] S/5240/Add. 2, May 21, 1963, p. 2. The official U.N. version of this whole question is summarized in the *Annual Report of the Secretary-General on the Work of the Organization: 16 June, 1962 to 15 June, 1963*, U.N. Doc A/5501, pp. 14-15.

prohibition was accepted by the Council and made explicit in the Assembly resolution of September 20, 1960, which called upon "all States to refrain from direct and indirect provision of arms and other material of war and military personnel" while the UNF remained in the Congo, "except upon the request of the United Nations." This view was reaffirmed in paragraph six of the November 24, 1961, Council resolution. While these resolutions were directed primarily toward states assisting Katanga, their legal implications were broader. Further, U.S. participation, though only through the provision of equipment, raised the question of direct big-power involvement, but perhaps no more so than previous U.S. logistical support of the U.N. operation.

The public announcement of the Greene Plan for military assistance from Belgium, Canada, Italy, Norway, Israel, and the United States under a U.N. umbrella drew criticism from several quarters. The Soviet Union challenged the Plan as a NATO scheme to impose colonial shackles upon the Congo. The United Arab Republic attacked the plan because of Israel's involvement. Some African leaders were distressed at Belgium's participation. All of this caused Thant to have second thoughts about the matter. On March 20, 1963, he discussed the Greene Plan with the Congo Advisory Committee which concluded that the urgently needed training of the ANC "could be most appropriately given" by the states which had contributed troops to the UNF. This advice ruled out the United States, Belgium, and Israel, and was probably meant to rule out Canada and Norway as well, both of which had sent only specialized personnel to the Congo. None of the neutralist states with troop contingents in the UNF offered such assistance. On April 29, 1963, Thant informed Adoula that he could not support the Plan. Adoula replied that the Congo as a sovereign state had the right to negotiate bilateral agreements and would do so. The Greene Plan as such was dead. Subsequent efforts to resuscitate it proved fruitless.

Adoula went ahead with bilateral military aid programs to train, modernize, and streamline the 35,000-man ANC. They were very slow in getting under way. The most colorful program was the paratroop training provided by Israel. By June 30, 1964, Israel had trained 220 paratroopers, including General Mobutu himself who made a publicity jump in the Army Day celebration in Leopoldville on November 17, 1963. By January 1965, a six-man Israeli military mission in Leopoldville was in the process of training the First Paracommando Battalion, already considered one of the Congolese army's best units. Since Mobutu regards the battalion as something of a personal security force, it was not expected to be deployed at any great distance from Leopoldville. For all practical purposes, Norway and Canada have not participated in the program. By June 30, 1964, Italy had just begun pilot training with twelve Congolese cadets.

The most significant program is the officer training effort conducted by Belgium. As of June 30, 1964, some seventy-five Belgian officers and advisers were in the Congo. Since independence, about 300 Congolese have gone to Belgium for military training. The slowness of the Belgian program in the Congo has been frequently criticized by Americans. It has many causes, among them the chaos within the country and the ANC, the inability to persuade qualified Belgian officers to volunteer, and the diverging Belgian and American views on an acceptable training plan for which the United States was expected to provide most of the equipment.

American Military Assistance

In practical and political terms, if not in legal terms, the U.S. bilateral aid program to the Congo, which started informally and quietly in October 1962, can be regarded as a supplement to and an extension of American support for the UNF. Both were motivated by the same objective—internal stability. Washington felt justified in establishing a three-man military mission in Leopoldville late in 1963, after the Secretary-General refused to go along with the Greene Plan or any other scheme for channeling and coordinating bilateral efforts.

The U.S. aid effort received a boost when Undersecretary of State W. Averell Harriman recommended, after a six-day tour of the Congo, March 26-31, 1964, that more ground vehicles, aircraft, and communications equipment should be sent. By June 30, 1964, the United States had contributed $6.1 million in bilateral assistance compared to $168.2 million in military assistance through the United Nations.[11] By that date, Washington had sent almost 100 military technicians to the Congo to train ANC troops in noncombat functions.[12] About a dozen Congolese officers have received training at Fort Knox, Kentucky. This training is part of a larger American program for emerging African states, one purpose of which is to develop "a cadre of strictly professional officers prepared to protect the legally constituted governments against subversion and domestic disorder."[13]

Responding to an urgent request from Prime Minister Adoula, Washington became more directly involved in the Central Government's effort to contain the Kivu revolt in June 1964. At that time, two or three Americans recruited by the Central Intelligence Agency (CIA) reportedly flew combat missions in Kivu Province until they were grounded by the State Department. Under contract with the Congo government, they had flown American-built T-28 fighters and attacked rebel positions near Bukavu. Six T-28s were reported to be in the Congo.[14] The Soviet Union referred to these fliers as colonialist "hirelings" of the CIA engaged in "punitive operations against Congolese patriots."[15] Subsequently, U.S. planes have been flown by Cuban pilots.

---

[11] UPI Dispatch, *New York Times*, June 22, 1964.

[12] Dan Kurzman, *Washington Post and Times Herald*, June 17, 1964.

[13] Defense Department announcement quoted by Fred S. Hoffman, AP Dispatch, *Washington Post and Times Herald*, July 6, 1963.

[14] Dan Kurzman, *Washington Post and Times Herald*, June 17 and 18, 1964. See also Bernard Gwertzman, *Evening Star* (Washington), June 17, 1964; and *New York Times*, June 17 and 18, 1964.

[15] U.N. Security Council, "Letter dated 6 July 1964 from the Permanent Representative of the Union of Soviet Socialist Republics addressed to the Secretary-General," Doc S/5798 (mimeographed, July 7, 1964).

The Phase-Out of the U.N. Force

The primary task of the UNF from the end of Katangan secession to its departure on June 30, 1964, was to maintain law and order, in cooperation with the ANC wherever feasible. As in earlier periods, the relationship between the U.N. command and General Mobutu ranged from hostile to tense. When the last UNF troops (58 Canadians and 85 Nigerians along with Major General Aguiyi Ironsi of Nigeria, the Force commander), left Leopoldville on June 30, not a single Congolese official went to the airport to pay his respects.[16] In the field, however, relations between UNF and ANC officers were occasionally cordial.

During this phase-out period, the UNF dropped from its peak of 19,782 in March 1963, to 6,535 the following December. It was reduced to zero on June 30, 1964. Some 400 Nigerian police, who had been serving in the Congo under the U.N. civilian administration, remained with the consent of the Central Government. The Nigerians had earned a good reputation for efficiently maintaining law and order.

As UNF units withdrew, the responsibility for each sector was transferred to an ANC officer. In February 1964, the UNF returned the Kitona and Kamina military bases to Belgium which held them under the 1960 Treaty. Brussels then turned them over to the Central Government.

For a variety of reasons, international interest in the Congo effort had dropped sharply with the end of Katangan secession in January 1963. Some of the neutralist states felt the job was completed with the "expulsion" of the Belgian "imperialists" and mercenaries from Katanga. They showed little interest in preserving law and order in the Congo or stability in Central Africa as such. In February 1963, both U.N. and U.S. officials had spoken of the end of the "military phase" of the mission. With this waning interest, it was not even certain that the

[16] AP Dispatch, *Washington Post and Times Herald*, July 1, 1964.

UNF would be continued beyond June 30, 1963, but the General Assembly on June 27 did extend it until the end of the year.

With persisting turbulence in the Congo, American Ambassador Gullion and officials in the State Department generally became convinced that the Force in reduced numbers should stay on for an additional six months. Eventually, Thant was persuaded to accept this view. On October 18, the Assembly voted to finance the UNF during the first half of 1964.

With such a short life expectancy and still operating under severe constraints against the use of force, a UNF commander would understandably seek to avoid clashes with lawless ANC units, ex-gendarmes, or marauding youth bands—to say nothing of involvement in armed revolts in three parts of the country. The Central Government did not ask the UNF for military aid to repulse or contain the rebels, but at its specific request, the United Nations and the United States did conduct rescue operations in rebel-infested areas.

Given the decreasing strength of the UNF, the psychology of disengagement within the Secretariat, and the continuing tension between U.N. officials and the Adoula government, it was inevitable that the Force would play a "caretaker role," to use Thant's words, during its last seventeen months in the Congo. Nevertheless, it was a positive role. In addition to assisting in rescue operations, the UNF helped to maintain law and order, to preserve the territorial integrity of the country, and to deter some tribal violence.

The peacekeeping effort had run its course. No government in the spring of 1964 urged the Security Council to undertake a new initiative to counter the threat to peace or to the territorial integrity of the Congo posed by the three insurrections encouraged and partly led by Red China. As of June 30, the rebels dominated areas totalling one-fifth of the Congo. Peking's Jenmin Jih Pao publicly hailed the "excellent revolutionary situation" in the Congo and expressed the hope that it would follow the pattern of the Communist war in South

Vietnam .[17] The insurgents were receiving some direction from the Chinese embassies in Congo (Brazzaville) and Burundi. The Central Government was incapable of dealing with the rebel challenge without external assistance. Such assistance to Prime Minister Adoula from African states or through the United Nations had little appeal to the ardent "anti-colonialists" who were primarily concerned with expelling Western "imperialists."

The United States continued its logistical support of the UNF to the end. As of June 30, 1964, the Defense Department had transported 118,091 troops and 18,596 tons of cargo into or out of the Congo, and airlifted 1,991 troops and 3,642 tons of cargo within the Congo. The breakdown follows:[18]

U.S. Airlift: 1960-64

Troops into the Congo	43,303
Troops out of the Congo	31,093
Cargo into the Congo (tons)	8,542
Cargo out of the Congo (tons)	1,904

U.S. Sealift: 1960-64

Troops into the Congo	20,352
Troops out of the Congo	23,343
Cargo into the Congo (tons)	5,322
Cargo out of the Congo (tons)	2,801

The Integration of Katanga

After the end of Katangan secession the major task of the Central Government, assisted by the United Nations, was to integrate the province, now divided into Katanga (southern area of the former province) and North Katanga, into the Republic of the Congo. The chief threat to order in these areas came from roving bands of Tshombe's former gendarmes

---

[17] *New York Times,* June 25, 1964.

[18] These statistics were provided by Captain William Alexander, USN, J-3, Joint Chiefs of Staff, Department of Defense, Sept. 16, 1964.

who were more interested in robbing and looting than in resisting integration. In March 1963, some 12,000 ex-gendarmes were still unaccounted for, but for economic reasons, by the time the UNF departed, probably most of them had returned to their villages, entered the civilian work force, or joined the ANC. A small hard core kept in touch with a nucleus of European mercenaries who were located across the border in Angola until Tshombe's return to the Congo on June 26, 1964. The UNF, in cooperation with Congolese authorities, dropped nearly 100,000 give-up-your-arms leaflets in March 1964, in a largely futile effort to flush out the remaining ex-gendarmes.

Occasionally, the UNF units, alone or with ANC units, went out into the bush looking for ex-gendarmes. These halfhearted and poorly organized efforts seldom yielded results.[19] For most of this period, the UNF also provided daily convoys from Elisabethville to the Northern Rhodesian border because of bandit activity in the area. The UNF cooperated with the police and the new ANC units being introduced into the provinces in maintaining order. The UNF helped to develop a working relationship between the Katangan police and the Congolese soldiers who regarded one another with suspicion.

Internal Security After Four Years

As of June 30, 1964, the prospect for political stability and internal security in the Congo was not reassuring. All observers, official and unofficial, had serious misgivings. Their appraisals were less optimistic than they had been just after the end of Katangan secession seventeen months before. One correspondent described the Congo as a "surrealistic nightmare." He added:

[19] In Elisabethville in November 1963, several competent observers told the author that the UNF was not eager to encounter any ex-gendarmes. On several occasions UNF officers were urged by U.S. authorities to make more patrols into the bush, but patrols were reluctant to leave the main roads.

The Congo is the place where the Defense Minister of the Republic creeps out of a mansion in besieged Bukavu in his stocking feet so he won't be heard leaving by the second-ranking officer in the Congolese Army . . . where heavily armed paracommandos flee before spear-toting tribesmen because they believe that the "anti-bullet-pills" concocted by witch doctors make the enemy indestructible.[20]

A *New York Times* editorial concluded that the "road to a genuinely free Congo appears stonier than ever."[21] Publicly, Secretary of State Dean Rusk said he did "not despair" and believed the Congolese leaders were capable of dealing with the crisis, but privately he had grave doubts.[22] Secretary-General Thant said the situation in 1963 had "incomparably improved," compared with 1960, but he acknowledged that the "immediate future" of the Congo was "none too promising."[23]

In spite of the political changes within the Congo during the first four years, a sober before-and-after analysis suggests that the fundamental internal security situation had neither significantly deteriorated nor significantly improved. At no time was the Central Government capable of maintaining law and order throughout the state. At all times, the Congolese government was weak, faction-ridden, inexperienced, bedeviled by corruption and assailed by tribal and provincial revolts. The constitutional foundation of the government, though somewhat strengthened with the advent of the Adoula government, remained shaky, and the rule of law was frequently ignored by all factions. The territorial integrity of the country was maintained and Katangan secession was ended, but these gains were partly offset by the existence of the three armed insurrections in 1964.

The replacement of the Communist-oriented Lumumba government of 1960 by the moderate and pro-Western Adoula

[20] Arnaud de Borchgrave, chief European correspondent, *Newsweek*, July 6, 1964, pp. 28 and 29.

[21] *New York Times,* July 1, 1964.

[22] *New York Times,* July 2, 1964.

[23] U.N. Security Council, Doc. S/5784, *op. cit.* (June 29, 1964), pp. 38 and 40.

government was perhaps the most important political development of the period. The eventual political coloration of the
controversial Tshombe government, created in July 1964, is
difficult to predict though, as of January 1965, the new Prime
Minister was following a moderate course.

If the Congo had a weak government and an unreliable
army after four years of U.N. peacekeeping, does this mean the
mission had failed? Even if it could be demonstrated that the
internal security situation was just as bad on the day the UNF
left as on the day it arrived (which is doubtful) this fact would
not prove the Force itself had failed. No one knows how much
worse (or better) the situation might have been if the Congolese government had received outside assistance elsewhere or
no outside assistance at all.

In assessing the role of the UNF, it is important to recognize
that the Congo drama was the product of many forces. Powerful internal factors—such as tribalism, political rivalry, untrained civil servants, illiteracy, and a widespread belief in
witchcraft, to say nothing of a weak and corrupt government,
an unreliable army, and disrupting economic forces—doubtless
had a greater impact on the Congo's destiny than the U.N.
military presence. External forces—including the policies of
the United States, Belgium, France, the Soviet Union, Red
China, and neutralist states of various shades; economic interests; and the total U.N. presence, including its efforts toward
political conciliation and other civilian activities—also played an
important role.

Though it was only one among many factors, the peacekeeping mission made a positive contribution to internal
stability. Thant's claim that the Force has been the "decisive
factor in preserving the territorial integrity" of the Congo,
"solely responsible for the cessation of the activities of the
mercenaries in Katanga" and "a major factor in preventing
wide-spread civil war," can be largely sustained by the record.[24]

The United Nations did not succeed in raising measurably

[24] *Ibid.*, p. 40.

the quality of the Congo army or in making any other provision for the maintenance of internal security. But the Secretary-General did not stand in the way of desperately needed bilateral military assistance requested by the Adoula government.

In terms of its objectives, the legal constraints upon its operations, its limited military capability, the magnitude of the problems it confronted, the U.N. Force performed well. It performed well, too, in spite of the lack of cooperation—and opposition—of the Soviet Union, France, Britain, and a number of smaller powers.

General Observations

1. After a number of abortive attempts by the U.N. command to assist in the training and reorganization of the Congolese army, it became clear that the Adoula government, and particularly General Mobutu, strongly preferred military assistance on a bilateral basis and from non-African states of its own choosing. Washington attempted to persuade the Secretary-General to have the United Nations serve as a channel and coordinator for the various bilateral training programs so that such aid would be in line with the Security Council prohibition against direct military assistance. Only when this effort failed, did the United States, Belgium, and Israel proceed with conventional bilateral military aid programs.

2. The bilateral military assistance programs got under way slowly and made little headway in improving the quality of the ANC which continued to be weak, disorganized, ill-disciplined, and lawless. The ANC not only failed to cope with any serious sizable disorders, but was itself a major source of disorder and instability. The absence of a reliable instrument of internal security continued to be a serious barrier to political cohesion and unity.

3. Official American and U.N. appraisals of the Congo situa-

tion as the last UNF troops withdrew on June 30, 1964, were considerably less optimistic than appraisals from the same spokesmen seventeen months before, just after Katangan secession had been ended. The fact that there was no significant improvement in the internal security picture after February 1963 indicates that Katangan secession was not responsible for the ills in the Congo as some neutralist and other spokesmen had believed. Secession was both a symptom and a cause of disunity and chaos in the country.

4. The loss of interest in the peacekeeping mission after the end of Katangan secession by some neutralist states suggests that their leaders were more concerned about threats to the authority and integrity of the newly independent Congo from the West than from the Communist bloc. To them secessionist Katanga was regarded largely as a Brussels-directed effort designed to frustrate successful decolonization. They showed little interest in the threats to the Central Government posed by the Moscow-supported rebel regime of Lumumba and Gizenga in Stanleyville or the Peking-supported movements in 1964. Yet both these rebel movements challenged the authority of Leopoldville, and the stability of the Congo, and jeopardized the prospects for peaceful change in Central Africa. The United States was concerned about threats to a unified Congo from all sources. But the State Department did not recommend that the UNF undertake any action to throw back or contain the 1964 revolts or that the Security Council consider any new measures to meet this less visible and subtler danger.

5

Operational Problems of the Force

*There is something eerie about the spectacle of the
United Nations having to plead and scrounge and
cajole to help tack together a minimal peacekeeping
force in the nick of time.*

HARLAN CLEVELAND, MARCH 21, 1964

MANY CONGOLESE regarded the United Nations Force
as an army of occupation, a resented foreign presence. This
was particularly true in Katanga. To any observer the external
appearance, behavior, and mood of the UNF resembled an
occupation army in a strange land. Some Congolese some of
the time welcomed the UNF as a protector. And many Congolese and European residents regarded the soldiers in blue berets
as a necessary evil.

The UNF troops lived a separate and parallel existence. They
had little contact with the African or European population.
They were supported from outside the country. The men
often displayed the boredom and impatience of combat troops
waiting for action or repatriation.

There were officers' clubs, recreation halls, Post Exchange
(PX) facilities selling American cigarettes and 35-millimeter
cameras, and even a UNF weekly, *Tom-Tom*.[1]

The UNF had many attributes of a regular army. In strength

---

[1] The March 21, 1962, issue of *Tom-Tom*, published in Leopoldville, carried
these stories: "Irish Players Arrive in Congo," "Brig. Goulson Dies in Crash,"
"Ethiopians 'A Bastion of Strength' says General," "Nigerian Troops, Police,
Hold Open Day in Leo," "Full Military Honors for 13 Italian Airmen,"
"U.N. Muslim Troops Observe Holy Month," and "On a Lion Shoot in
Katanga."

it approximated a division. There were combat battalions. There were soldiers equipped with automatic rifles. The few lightly armored vehicles carried the familiar blue olive branch and globe symbol of the world organization in place of national markings. The UNF had a small air force which included jet fighters. During its four years, more than 93,000 officers and men from thirty-five nations served in the Force. Each wore his national military uniform and a U.N. arm insignia.

Appearances to the contrary, the UNF was not a combat army, an occupation army, or an army at all in any conventional sense. The UNF had no enemy. Its object was peace and order, not victory. Yet it needed a greater military capability than a normal police force because it was assailed by a military force in Katanga and was deployed among warring tribes. As a substitute internal security force, the UNF at times had no clearly recognized law to defend or order to uphold. And it even lacked some of the powers of a regular police establishment.

Operating largely under the provisions of Chapter VI of the U.N. Charter, the peaceful settlement force in the Congo was an intentionally hobbled, and hence widely misunderstood, army. It was severely limited by the political constraints placed upon it by the Security Council. Even after the Council broadened its authority, the UNF could employ force only in self-defense, to prevent civil war, and to apprehend foreign mercenaries. Because of the added political constraints— chiefly the necessity for the consent of the host state for any significant operation and the reservations of the governments donating troops—the UNF did not use the full legal mandate authorized by the Council. In justifying Round Three, which succeeded in ending Katangan secession, Thant invoked only the authority to use force in self-defense and the right of freedom of movement for the UNF.

The Force in the Congo was improvised from the beginning. Its mandate was vague, uncertain, and shifting. Its mission was novel. The theater in which it operated was chaotic. The sources of its manpower and material support were not assured.

And at all times various factions within the Congo and certain governments outside the Congo sought to use, neutralize, or subvert the operations of the UNF.

The UNF was not the instrument of a single political will. It was not the coercive arm of a government. It was the instrument of a coalition of states with different and frequently opposing interests in the Congo and in the larger world. The integrity of the operation depended to a considerable extent upon the skill of the Secretary-General who, on one side, was assailed with conflicting advice from interested governments, and, on the other, had to rely upon officers and troops from many states to carry out his interpretation of the mandate. These officers and men represented important differences in military tradition, military doctrine, staff procedure, training, pay scales, equipment, language, and food habits—to say nothing of cultural, political, and educational differences. Furthermore, the tours of duty for both officers and troop contingents were too short. This was true even at the top. In four years, there were five different Force commanders of five different nationalities.

Given these unusual circumstances, it would not be fair to judge the operations of the UNF by standards appropriate to a conventional army on a conventional mission of comparable size and scope. Nor would it be fair to judge the efficiency of the UNF by standards appropriate to an identical mission entrusted to a competent military establishment of a single government, such as the American or British armies. So judged, the performance of the UNF would rate from fair to poor.

Operational efficiency is not the most appropriate standard for measuring the performance of any internationally authorized peacekeeping mission. The central question is: how well did the operation succeed in serving its assigned mission and at what political cost? Nevertheless, operational efficiency is not an irrelevant consideration. Efficiency factors such as speed and financial cost are related to political cost. And political cost is related to the political objective of a mission. This explains the interest of the Secretariat and governments supporting the Congo effort in evaluating the efficiency of UNF performance especially as such an evaluation may contain lessons applicable to possible future operations.

Problems of the Force

In analyzing the problems of the UNF it is essential to distinguish between those rooted in the nature of any internationally authorized nonsanctions operation and those which are correctable without any fundamental change in the international political context. The major obstacles to military efficiency are clearly derived from political constraints. The evaluation in this chapter is concerned only with correctable weaknesses, and not with weaknesses which might be eliminated by drastic changes in the character or alignment of international politics. Nevertheless, the question of adequacy should be raised despite its political overtones. In physical terms, the Force did not have a clear preponderance of combat power in Katanga. Its armament was limited to infantry heavy weapons and its tactical transportation resources were strained. Had the full capabilities of Tshombe's military potential been employed, U.N. losses in men and equipment would have been much higher than they were. The possible political impact of greater, or sustained casualties casts some doubt on the validity of the decisions which limited the Force in size and performance. As events developed in Katanga, the price of weakness fortunately did not have to be paid.

The UNF faced all the problems of traditional military policing operations. The analysis here will focus on the difficulties encountered in the Congo effort. Some of these difficulties have characterized all U.N. peaceful settlement missions. The following enumeration of problems is based upon many interviews with U.N. civilian and military officials (including four of the five Force commanders and two of the three commanders in Katanga) and with diplomats and others who observed or participated in the operation. Among the published sources consulted, none was more helpful than an address by Major General Indar Jit Rikhye, the military adviser to the Secretary-General.[2]

COMMAND AND CONTROL. The normal problems of command were complicated by the quick deployment of the Force without prior planning, the necessity to buy or borrow essential communications equipment, the confused mandate, the political constraints, and the requirement for working with officers and troops from many states. In the complex and changing Congo, the lines of authority among the Secretary-General, the officer in charge and the Force commander in Leopold-ville, and the civilian representative and field commander in Elisabethville were not as carefully defined as they might have been, which resulted in needless chaos and inefficiency.

In two major incidents (described in Chapter 3), subordinates took action not authorized by U.N. Headquarters. One was Conor Cruise O'Brien's controversial attempt to end Katanga's secession by apprehending mercenaries and Katangan ministers in Elisabethville on September 13, 1961. In this situation Hammarskjold appeared to have lost control of the operation for a brief period. The other incident was Brigadier R. S. Noronha's crossing of the Lufira River on his way to Jadotville in early January 1963. There was no loss of control here. The O'Brien incident, which has not yet been fully explained, had much more severe political repercussions than the latter, largely, perhaps, because it was unsuccessful. As far as can be ascertained, there was no serious case of insubordination during the four years. Several Force commanders, on the other hand, have complained about occasional unnecessary interference on the part of the Secretary-General or insufficient authority to make military decisions in the field.

One of the most difficult and persistent problems was the

[2] "Preparation and Training of United Nations Peace-Keeping Forces," prepared for delivery at a private conference on U.N. Security Forces, Oslo, Norway, Feb. 21, 1964 (mimeographed—Adelphi Paper No. 9, Institute for Strategic Studies, London, 1964).

inefficiency, waste, confusion, and tension resulting from an unsatisfactory relationship between the Congo military operation and the U.N. Field Operations Service.[3] The lack of cooperation, coordination, and even communication between the UNF command and the Office of General Services was described as "atrocious" by a high Secretariat officer. The Field Service was assigned the responsibility for the supply and support of both civilian and military operations in the Congo. As far as the UNF command was concerned, this meant a duplication of effort at all levels and constant jurisdictional confusion. This confusion adversely affected logistical support, inventory control, movement control, accounting, the disposal of surplus material, and the general efficiency of the operation.

QUALITY CONTROL. One of the major problems emphasized by the Force commanders was the lack of fully qualified officers, specialized units, and regular troops. There was also, it must be added, a wide range in quality among the Force commanders themselves.

Some national troop contingents were good. Others were not. The Secretary-General accepted underqualified troops for several reasons. The necessity for haste and the desire to have a variety of politically acceptable states represented led to the acceptance of some poorly trained or ill-disciplined contingents. Some donor states had low quality military establishments and their best was not good enough. Other states with qualified troops were reluctant to send their best when they had more pressing national requirements elsewhere. Still other states had laws which prevented their sending regular army units outside the country; hence, they recruited inadequately trained volunteers for the UNF. The efficiency of some units was reduced because their government insisted on a six-month tour of duty rather than a year.

[3] The Field Operations Service was established in 1949 in accordance with a General Assembly resolution. Its purpose is to provide technical support for U.N. activities throughout the world. It functions as a part of the Office of General Services.

The quality of some specialized units, especially those of mixed nationality, was poor. Things were particularly bad in multinational air transport units designed to facilitate the heavy traffic in personnel and cargo. According to one U.N. commander, these units included men with different levels of specialized training, ranging from reasonable efficiency to total ignorance. Inadequate knowledge of the working language, English, further reduced the efficiency of these units. In contrast, Major General Rikhye has pointed to the efficiency of the Canadian air transport unit in UNEF which has operated with "no organizational difficulties."[4]

The UNF has had a number of outstanding staff officers. Others ranged from average to poor. This is understandable because the Secretary-General had to rely on the good judgment and good faith of the donor government. While he was occasionally in the happy position of being able to request a well-qualified officer by name, this was not the rule. Usually, he had to request a government to nominate an officer; in these circumstances it would have been awkward to reject the nominee. Further, it was probably more difficult to replace an unqualified man in the UNF than in a well-run national army. There were cases where poor officers continued in the Congo for a second or third tour of duty. It was virtually impossible for the Force commander to dismiss them against the wishes of their national contingent commander.

MILITARY DISCIPLINE.   The normally difficult job of maintaining strict discipline was made more difficult by the variety of military codes represented in the Force and by the fact that a soldier was ultimately accountable not to the U.N. commander but to his national contingent commander. Only the latter had the authority to discipline him. The fact that the contingent commander alone could submit confidential performance reports on U.N. military personnel created a situation where men or officers employed in multinational staff positions became more concerned with impressing their contingent

[4] Rikhye, op. cit., p. 8.

commanders than in supporting the staff commander. This is understandable because the contingent commander not only had more authority over a subordinate national, but also the power to block or facilitate his military career. The situation of dual authority did not necessarily lead to dual loyalties, but it encouraged indiscipline or lack of loyalty to the United Nations where there was a predisposition to react in this way. Fortunately, the great majority of officers were loyal to the Force and most cases of crime and indiscipline were dealt with properly by the contingent commanders. According to Major General Rikhye, however, there were a "few cases, including major crimes, in which the governments concerned were not disposed to make the necessary investigations and to take suitable disciplinary action against the culprits. The impact of the attitude on the reputation, discipline, and morale of a U.N. force" and on the host government was a serious matter.[5]

TROOP MORALE.   The morale of U.N. soldiers in the Congo was adversely affected not only by the uneven and inequitable application of military discipline, but also by the wide variations in national pay and allowance scales. Donor states paid regular salaries and overseas allowances to their men and officers in accordance with their own laws and regulations. This resulted in striking contrasts in which two men doing the same job and taking the same risks were being paid by their governments on completely different scales. An Indian private, for example, received a monthly salary of $25 and an overseas allowance of $8, while his Swedish comrade received a salary of about $270 and an overseas allowance of $120. This wide discrepancy between $33 and $390 reflects the general economic disparity between India and Sweden, though it must be said that an Indian major probably enjoys a higher social and economic status in his country than a Swedish major does in his.

While the United Nations could do nothing about these basic national salary and allowance differences, it did attempt to

[5] *Ibid.,* p. 7.

equalize the situation in the Congo by providing each man and officer, regardless of nationality, with a daily allowance of $1.30 for his personal needs. With this monthly income of $39.60 in local Congolese currency, he could buy small items at the UN-PX. Large purchases, such as cameras, had to be paid in a hard currency and required special approval. At the end of his tour of duty, any member of the UNF was permitted to convert up to 50 percent of his accumulated daily allowance into a hard currency.

In accordance with General Assembly resolutions, the donor governments required the United Nations to reimburse them for the overseas allowance they paid their men while in the Congo. Some governments, notably Sweden, also required reimbursement for the salaries of their men and officers. All Swedes serving in the UNF were mercenaries and not members of the Swedish Army. Thus, in direct costs, the United Nations paid $390 a month for a Swedish soldier and $8 for an Indian soldier. But this is not the whole story. The United Nations, while not paying the salary of an Indian in the Congo, was required to reimburse the Indian government for the salaries and equipment of reserve units called up to replace some of the regular Indian troops in the Congo. Hence, the statement that the cost to the United Nations of one dollar is "about $8 a month and the other $625"[6] appears to be incorrect on both counts. Adding the daily U.N. allowance, the Swedish soldier would cost $430 a month and the Indian soldier $48 *plus* the indirect costs of replacing him by a fully equipped reservist in India in those cases where he was replaced. There are no available figures on the cost per man of these indirect obligations to the Indian government.

Morale was also adversely affected by inadequate recreational facilities, rest leaves, and medical facilities, and the black-market operations of some U.N. troops in PX supplies. Black-market American cigarettes were peddled openly on the streets.

[6] *Ibid.*, p. 7.

Dissatisfaction also resulted from unequal accommodation for headquarters officers of different nationalities.

HEALTH. Although the health of the troops was generally good, there were problems due to inadequate medical facilities in some areas and the absence of proper field latrines, cook houses, and bathing facilities in others. Some contingents came to the Congo without proper clothing, cooking equipment, or inoculations against tropical diseases. Some troops arrived with latent diseases and had to be sent back.

COMMUNICATIONS. Generally, military communications were satisfactory. The facilities were technically adequate, but since the Force and civil administration had to use the same network, important messages were sometimes delayed. Cipher facilities usually were adequate, but during Round Three in Katanga, according to a U.N. report, the system was overburdened by an unnecessary number of classified messages. During this operation, U.S. communication between the field and New York was faster than U.N. communication, resulting in at least one instance where American officials in New York informed Secretariat officials of UNF developments which had not yet been reported to them.

LANGUAGE. For practical reasons English was selected as the official language of Congo civilian and military operations. Though reasonable English facility was a requirement for every officer and NCO, the fact that many men did not have a satisfactory mastery of the language resulted in some confusion and inefficiency. Referring to the officers at the U.N. headquarters in Elisabethville for whom English was a second language, O'Brien observed:

> Most of them were liable to assume they knew English perfectly, but in fact, in a university-level examination in oral English, they would have ranged from 80 per cent down to about 15 per cent. In the lower ranges this could lead to serious factual misunderstanding; in the higher ranges to the subtler strains of misplaced

emphasis. . . . The trouble here was no more than a steady friction, but it involved some loss of efficiency.[7]

INTERNAL TRANSPORTATION AND MOVEMENT CONTROL. Transportation of troops, weapons, and other cargo over the vast area of the Congo would have posed problems for a competent national military force. For the hastily assembled UNF it was an especially formidable task. The volume of internal airlift was considerable, and it is in this area that the most serious weaknesses were revealed. During the period from May 1962 to August 1963, the internal airlift averaged seven million pounds of cargo and nine thousand personnel a month. There was also a need for observation, reconnaissance, evacuation, and rescue operations involving a variety of aircraft. Combat missions were flown in Katanga.

The UNF suffered from lack of aircraft, supporting equipment, and qualified personnel. Many of the ground personnel, says Major General Rikhye, "were found wanting in suitable qualifications. There were instances of erroneous recruitment, e.g., a man recruited to fill a vacancy in a definite trade had no previous experience or training. Difficulties were also encountered in obtaining personnel in accounting, requisitioning, and issuance of spare parts. There was also a serious lack of suitable personnel who could supervise air loading to ensure that most economical use of aircraft was made."[8]

Since the United Nations did not maintain a large civilian or military air fleet, it had to charter commercial aircraft from time to time, and on at least one occasion with unhappy results. A private American air carrier was chartered to repatriate U.N. troops in 1964, but it performed so poorly that the contract was cancelled after only a small portion of the job had been completed.

During Round Three in Katanga, the UNF command requested airlift support from the American government. In

[7] Conor Cruise O'Brien, *To Katanga and Back* (Simon and Schuster, 1962), pp. 252-53.
[8] Rikhye, *op. cit.*, p. 9.

response, the U.S. Air Force provided three C-124s with American crews to perform the designated task on a cost reimbursable basis. The Air Force also provided a tanker plane. This was a highly satisfactory operation.

On the ground, the UNF also had serious transportation problems because of the lack of spare parts, repair manuals, maintenance facilities, and qualified drivers and mechanics. The problem was aggravated by the great variety of vehicles. At one point there were some 3,000 vehicles of nearly ninety different makes and types. The maintenance, repair, and provision of spare parts for this number and variety was an impossible task, so at one point the Force commander declared 1,300 of the nonstandard types obsolete. "The general standard of mechanical transport maintenance and driving has been poor amongst most contingents" and the "accident rate in the U.N. forces has tended to be high."[9]

The air movement control units, as noted above, suffered in efficiency because of unqualified personnel and the language problem.

LOGISTICAL SUPPORT.   The great bulk of the logistical support for the Congo operation was provided by the United States at the request of the Secretary-General on a cost reimbursable basis. Washington designated the U.S. Air Force as the executive agent within the Department of Defense to perform this and related services. This indispensable assistance was accomplished efficiently and to the satisfaction of both parties.

There were, however, delays and waste due to the inefficiency of U.N. administrative machinery occasioned in part by the confused relationship between the UNF command and the Field Operations Service. According to American military officers, millions of dollars could have been saved with a modest amount of planning. This is particularly true with respect to the unnecessary airlifting of men and supplies when they could have been transported by sea. Vehicles, weapons, and am-

[9]*Ibid.,* p. 6.

munition were not properly inventoried and maintained. With good management, it is estimated that transportation costs could have been cut by as much as 50 percent.

Further inefficiency resulted from the fact that many requests to the United States for supplies were either so tardy or so vague that they could not be filled properly. Sometimes the requests made no sense at all. On January 7, 1963, for example, the Field Operations Service requested the State Department to provide 532,831 rounds of various calibers. U.S. military officers questioned the request since a recent shipment had been made and since the period of active hostilities appeared to have ended. Major General Rikhye's office, at the insistence of an American officer, cabled the Force commander in Leopoldville, asking that the ammunition order be related to actual stocks and anticipated needs. This resulted in a modified request cutting the original order in half. Further inquiry from New York resulted in the cancellation of the order entirely.

INTELLIGENCE.   For political reasons, the United Nations was sensitive about the word "intelligence," so military intelligence operations in the Congo were carried on under the Military Information Branch. The UNF was hampered in this work by too few qualified specialists and too little equipment, especially for aerial photography and for recording Katanga radio broadcasts. A major problem was the lack of funds to buy information. As a result, intelligence was often slow or spotty. In spite of these limitations, however, the UNF was able to obtain, mainly by aerial reconnaissance, adequate information on the location of all Katangan aircraft so they could be destroyed on the ground at the beginning of Round Three. During that operation the UNF also secured valuable intelligence by improvised interception of radio traffic in Katanga.

PUBLIC INFORMATION.   Though the United Nations was not waging war in the Congo, it found itself the victim of psychological warfare and inflammatory attacks by the Katanga propaganda apparatus both in the Congo and throughout the world. In the Congo itself, the United Nations was unable to respond adequately to hostile propaganda or to present its case to the African or European population partly because of a self-imposed inhibition against a public information effort and partly because the information program was directed more toward the morale of UNF troops than toward the population. The effort also suffered because of the lack of qualified personnel, the confused political situation, and the unprecedented nature of the mission. As the UNF gained experience, it improved in presenting its story. One ironic incident, mentioned in Chapter 3, illustrated the perils of an increased public relations consciousness. In order to correct the "bad press" which the United Nations felt it received in Rounds One and Two, Major General Prem Chand invited the press to accompany his troops during Round Three. As a result, the killing of the two Belgian women in a Volkswagen by U.N. troops outside of Jadotville was dramatically reported to the world by word and photograph.

Readiness and Operational Efficiency

Taking into account its fundamental nature and the political constraints upon it, the performance of the UNF in the Congo was good. A peacekeeping mission must be judged primarily by how well it fulfills its political purpose and only secondarily by its military efficiency. Nevertheless, efficiency is a relevant consideration.

A distinction should be made between readiness and operational efficiency. Readiness is the capacity to deploy a mission efficiently and on short notice. Operational efficiency has to do with the cost of carrying out a mission. Readiness is important, because a speedy response to a local crisis may contain the problem before it gets out of hand. Further, the knowledge that the Secretary-General has the capacity to move quickly may deter certain small threats or breaches of the peace. The

Congo experience, as well as the other peacekeeping missions, indicates that both readiness and operational efficiency can be enhanced without a radical change in international politics, and that the same measures contribute to both objectives.

Many of the measures for upgrading readiness and efficiency suggested below have been advocated by U.N. officials or by spokesmen of friendly governments, such as the United States, Canada, and the Scandinavian states.[10] Some of the more detailed suggestions were developed in a previous study in which the present writer was involved.[11] Any of these proposals, if adopted, would help to correct some of the weaknesses and mitigate some of the problems encountered in the Congo.

Prior Planning vs. Improvisation

In theory, a permanent U.N. force is the most efficient peacekeeping instrument, but a militarily significant standing army is neither feasible nor desirable in the near future. A U.N. military establishment capable of fielding a ten-thousand-man force and independent of the control of any state or

---

[10] There is a remarkable consensus among U.N. officials, statesmen, military officers who have served in peacekeeping missions, and scholars of the problem on the major next steps to be taken. This consensus was expressed at an off-the-record International Conference on United Nations Security Forces held in Oslo, Norway, February 21-22, 1964, which included sixty participants from fifteen countries. The views expressed at the Ottawa Peacekeeping Conference, November 2-6, 1964, were in substantial accord with those of the Oslo Conference. The Canadian Conference, called by Prime Minister Lester B. Pearson, was restricted to official delegates from governments which had provided troops for peacekeeping efforts.

Especially important among statements by U.N. officials are: Rikhye, *op. cit.;* U Thant, "A United Nations Stand-By Peace Force" (U.N. Press Release SG/1520, June 12, 1963); and Brian E. Urquhart, "United Nations Peace Forces and the Changing United Nations," *International Organization,* Vol. XVII (Spring 1963), pp. 338-54.

[11] Institute for Defense Analyses, *National Armaments and International Force* (IDA HQ, Final Report R-101, Study DAIS, 1963). See especially pp. xi-xx and 51-74.

group of states would be impossible to create without a drastic change in both the structure and alignments of contemporary international politics. To maintain such a force, the United Nations would require attributes of sovereignty which its member states, both great and small, have shown no disposition to grant it. Among these attributes would be the legal right to:

1. Secure necessary manpower from states.

2. Secure necessary financial support.

3. Enforce discipline among members of the force and protect them from any actions by governments which would infringe upon their rights or responsibilities as members of the force.

4. Requisition property, facilities, and services from states and exercise jurisdiction over these assets.

The political infeasibility of a large standing force does not necessarily mean that a very small permanent corps of military officers trained in specialized observation or inspection functions would be impossible to create. It is noteworthy, however, that even this modest instrumentality has not been seriously advanced by Secretariat or government officials. In fact, the idea of a standing force of any size has been consistently opposed.[12]

There are two major ways of deploying a temporary force: *improvisation* to meet a specific crisis or some degree of *prior planning* to meet a variety of likely crises. The U.N. missions to date have all been improvised; there was no prior planning either for the recruiting of troops or specialized personnel or for sending them into the field. Each peacekeeping effort has been unique, and, despite its ad hoc nature, each has been reasonably successful. This fact suggests that there is a certain prac-

---

[12] See Harlan Cleveland, "The Practical Side of Peacekeeping," *Bulletin,* U.S. Department of State, Vol. 46 (April 9, 1962), pp. 585-86. U Thant also takes this view. See his "A United Nations Stand-By Peace Force," *op. cit.*

tical value to improvisation. An ad hoc response to a Security Council resolution can be tailored to meet the specific requirements of the mission: political, military, geographic, or racial. Prior planning, particularly the stockpiling of equipment or overdependence upon a few earmarked general-purpose units, introduces an undesirable element of rigidity into the situation.

Although there will probably be future ad hoc missions and though these efforts may be effective, partly because of improvisation, there is general agreement that both readiness and operational efficiency would be enhanced by some degree of planning. Such planning can take place in four areas: administration, recruitment of men and officers, financing, and the functions of a U.N. military staff. Each will be considered in turn.

Alternative Ways of Administering a Force

All U.N. peacekeeping forces have been directed by the Secretary-General. This has worked reasonably well, but the Congo operation consumed such a large portion of the Secretary-General's energy and of the resources of the entire Organization that alternative ways of administration should be seriously studied.

In the Korean operation (which involved a sanctions force as opposed to a peaceful settlement force), the United States served as the executive agent for the United Nations, providing both political direction and military command. This arrangement, admittedly under political circumstances quite different from those that led to the UNEF and Congo efforts, nevertheless suggests one possible type of administration which merits further exploration; namely, the use of one state as a U.N. instrument to fulfill certain specific executive and administrative functions. In West New Guinea, Pakistan alone provided the 1,500-man Security Force which was administered by the U.N. Temporary Executive Authority under the direction of the Secretary-General. The United States and Canada made a composite air unit available.

Under certain political circumstances in the future, the Secretary-General might designate an acceptable government to police a truce, patrol a border, or keep the peace in a specified area in accordance with the objectives and constraints laid down by a Council or Assembly resolution. Single-government administration of such an effort under the political control of the Secretary-General, while not free of difficulties, would introduce a degree of efficiency not possible when personnel of many states are involved in management. One variation of this executive agent approach would be to give an acceptable government full responsibility for one major function of a mission. Washington, for example, might have been given the sole responsibility for logistical support in the Congo.

Single-government administration will work successfully, however, only when the executive agent remains true to its mandate and is politically acceptable to the parties most concerned. The impartial nature of the operation needs to be preserved, but it is important to recognize that the international character of a peacekeeping mission depends not so much on the multinational makeup of its personnel and administration as on the legitimacy of the authority from which it derives its mandate. A responsible executive agent would be guided by the instructions of the Council, the General Assembly, the advice of the Secretary-General, and the views of the states most directly involved.

Unit and Capability Earmarking

In the past several years, Canada, the Scandinavian states, the Netherlands, Italy, New Zealand, and Iran have taken small steps toward earmarking units or specialized military personnel for possible U.N. peacekeeping duties. The United States, for example, has repeatedly stated its intention to provide logistical support for future operations, but it has been understood that this would apply only when such operations were consistent with its national interests. Other states have also indicated their willingness to support peacekeeping efforts with the same reservation.

The readiness and operational efficiency of the United Nations would be further enhanced if additional states would pledge troops or specialized capabilities for future use. As Major General Rikhye has pointed out, such voluntarily earmarked units would be "under complete command and control of their government prior to their use by the United Nations" and there would be "no financial responsibility for the U.N. during the stand-by phase."[13] With such pledges of assistance the Secretary-General could build up a capability inventory to be called upon in an emergency. The larger and more varied the inventory the better. The Congo experience indicates the need for airlift, sealift, communications, combat units trained and equipped for riot control duties, administrative staff, transportation, maintenance, supply, and other service support units. The U.N. military staff could develop what might be called a shopping list and invite appropriate governments to make their pledges accordingly.

The Secretary-General cannot demand a legally or politically binding pledge of troops or specialized personnel from a potential donor state. In fact, he should encourage such a state to specify its reservations. For example, an African government may stipulate that its troops may not fire against the troops of another African state, except in self-defense. Another state might specify that no more than one thousand of its troops may be committed to a U.N. force at any one time. Whether reservations are specified or not, it would be understood by all concerned that a donor government would withhold its pledged assistance if its national interests so require.

The larger the capability inventory, the greater the probability of finding politically acceptable and militarily qualified

---

[13] Rikhye, op. cit., p. 4.

units and personnel to do the job. The capability inventory need not be highly formalized. When a specific request for help has been made in the past, interested states have offered assistance even though they had made no prior pledges. In the Congo, thirty-four outside states provided some kind of assistance.

Pledged units would require little or no special U.N. training or orientation before they were called upon by the United Nations, though they would need to be briefed carefully on the special requirements of the mission before taking up their duties in the field. In the case of some specialized units a more thorough indoctrination may be desirable. The main requirement is that each unit perform its function well and obey the orders of the U.N. command, even though these orders may place unusual restraints upon it. The training of senior officers is a different matter and will be discussed below.

The Financial Problem

The financing of U.N. peacekeeping operations involving military forces is not fundamentally an economic or legal problem, but rather a political problem. If there were sufficient political consensus for supporting a given effort, there would be no serious monetary questions. In an international environment of conflicting interests, the financial problem will focus on ways to achieve an equitable and timely sharing of costs which will facilitate rather than hamstring the deployment of peacekeeping missions.

The financial problem embraces two basic principles which cannot always be reconciled—the principle of collective responsibility and the principle of safeguarding the interests of member states. Collective responsibility for keeping the peace is central to the U.N. system, and the organization could hardly justify its existence if this principle were surrendered. Collective responsibility for the "expenses of the Organization" is written into the Charter and has been upheld in principle as applicable to peacekeeping costs. Yet, if a state cannot be legally obligated to contribute men or material to a U.N. force, should the General Assembly have the authority to compel that state to contribute financially to a particular mission it believes is detrimental to its interests?[14]

Reflecting these two principles, the financing of peacekeeping operations to date has not followed consistently either the assessment or the voluntary approach. The Congo effort combined them both. The failure of France and the Soviet Union to pay their assessed shares of the Congo operation has been the chief cause of the monetary difficulties of the Organization which came to a head in 1962. As of early 1965, the financial problem had not been settled, but the majority of members, led by the United States, continued to insist that the payment of past peacekeeping expenditures was mandatory and that the accumulation of two years arrears was sufficient cause under Article 19 for denying a delinquent member a vote in the Assembly.

The complexity of these fiscal questions suggests that the flexible and pragmatic approach expressed by the United States in 1963 may be wiser than the quest for a single formula applicable to all situations. In the Working Group of Twenty-one established by the Assembly to deal with this question the United States said:

> In the foreseeable future no single formula or single set of principles or criteria can be applied to any and all peacekeeping operations. The method of financing of each peacekeeping operation should be dealt with as it occurs, learning from each operation what may be desirable for the future and adjusting each solution to the particular facts of the case.[15]

Acknowledging that the problem results from political conflict, the capacity of the United Nations to underwrite peace-

[14] This dilemma is discussed in detail in John G. Stoessinger, *Financing the United Nations System* (Brookings Institution, 1964). See especially pp. 100-90.

[15] U.N. General Assembly, "Financing of U.N. Peacekeeping Operations: Report of the Working Group on the Examination of the Administrative and Budgetary Procedures of the U.N." Doc. A/5407 (March 29, 1963), p. 9.

keeping operations would be enhanced by three measures that could be taken by the General Assembly:

1. Include in the budget of the United Nations, as a regular expenditure for Secretariat services, support for a small increase in the present military staff. Also include in the budget the costs of any agreed-upon officer training program and any other staff or program connected with the permanent peacekeeping requirements of the Organization, as distinguished from the requirements of a specific operation.

2. Establish by regular assessment or by voluntary contribution or a combination of both a special contingency fund of perhaps $50 million, to be available only for the immediate needs of newly authorized peacekeeping missions. Such a fund would permit some breathing space for grappling with arrangements to finance each new mission, the budget of which would provide for repaying the money drawn from the contingency fund. The establishment and operation of such a fund is far more complex and controversial than the inclusion of an enlarged military staff within the U.N. budget.

At the present time, the Secretary-General, under the annual Assembly resolution on unforeseen and extraordinary expenditures, is authorized to commit up to $2 million (and with the approval of the Advisory Committee on Administrative and Budgetary Questions, up to $10 million) to reimburse the states involved in initial arrangements for any approved peacekeeping operation.

3. Establish a special finance committee, similar in composition to the Working Group of Twenty-one. This committee would consider various ways of underwriting peacekeeping operations, "including direct financing by countries involved in a dispute, voluntary contributions, and assessed contributions;" it would make recommendations to the Assembly on how to pay for a given operation. These recommendations would take into account the political interests of members, their varied capacities to pay, and other factors. Such a proposal embodying the principle of flexibility, together with other recommenda-

tions, was laid before the Working Group by the United States on September 14, 1964.[16]

The Military Advisory Staff

To assist him in dealing with rapidly unfolding events in the Congo, the Secretary-General secured the services of a military adviser. He later provided the adviser with a small supporting staff. Major General Rikhye has headed this staff of one colonel and two majors. If the staff were continued and gradually enlarged to perhaps ten or twelve officers, and if its functions were correspondingly enlarged, it could increase considerably the readiness and operational efficiency of any peacekeeping missions authorized in the future.

In performing its two central functions—advising on any current operations and contingency planning for future missions—the major resources available to the staff would reside not within the Secretariat, but in governments that support the concept and practice of peacekeeping missions. Because of its cost and political implications, the United Nations cannot and should not have a complete planning staff similar to a large national military establishment. What is required is a small but competent group of people who know where to go for assistance. In short, the advisory staff should serve primarily as a coordinating body between the Secretary-General and the governments willing to provide the necessary resources. In this modest rule the staff could engage in a variety of specific functions, most of which have not been carried out adequately —if at all—in the past. For some of these functions, the staff would cooperate with the Office of General Services and other offices of the Secretariat.

[16] U.N. General Assembly, "Financing of United Nations Peacekeeping Operations," Working Paper submitted by the delegation of the United Nations to the Working Group on the Examination of the Administrative and Budgetary Procedures of the United Nations, Doc. A/AC.113/30 (September 14, 1964), p. 3.

1. INFORMATION GATHERING.   The need for pertinent information about any future operation is obvious, but this need cannot be met, even with a larger military staff, by stockpiling vast quantities of fast-decaying data on every likely contingency. Only wealthy governments have the necessary resources to do this. A U.N. staff could, however, operate a reference and map room stocked with reliable permanent information. The staff should secure the bulk of its information from readily available sources supplemented by the experience of its officers, by occasional staff visits to the general areas of potential peacekeeping missions and to potential donor states. The staff would also profit from improved liaison arrangements with national military establishments. Identifying reliable sources from which current information could be quickly gained should be one of the primary tasks of the staff. During the entire Congo operation, the U.N. military staff depended heavily upon the United States and other cooperating governments for information.

2. OPERATIONAL PLANNING.   The first task of operational planning is to develop detailed and yet flexible shopping lists of troops, specialized units, equipment, logistical support, and other requirements for probable future missions. These lists could be quickly adapted to meet the unique requirements of a specific crisis. The staff should also prepare or arrange for the preparation of standard operating procedures, checklists, manuals (see below), standing instructions, directives, etc., covering all areas of operational responsibility. Among the arrangements the staff could undertake in cooperation with the Office of General Services are these:

Overflight and Facility Rights: Quietly negotiate in advance comprehensive agreements for contingent rights for overflight, use of ports, refueling, communications, etc., with all governments prepared to cooperate. These standby agreements would not, of course, automatically come into effect upon the request of the Secretary-General. The government would have the option of noncooperation for political or other reasons.

Air and Sea Transportation: Compile an inventory of air and shipping companies competent to perform anticipated services and large enough to release some of their capacity on short notice. The United Nations should then enter into standby contracts with such companies. Similar standby arrangements should also be made with appropriate governments.

Fuel and Lubrication: Negotiate standby contracts with major worldwide oil companies for fuel and lubrication.

Materiel: Although no stockpiling of arms, food, or other equipment is feasible because of cost and obsolescence, the staff should seek to develop standardized lists of arms, surface vehicles, communications gear, and other essential equipment; they should be able to identify sources from which such supplies can be readily obtained.

3. DEVELOPING THE CAPABILITY INVENTORY. In the light of anticipated needs for troops and specialized units, the staff should assist the Secretary-General in securing the pledges of support from member states. As military men they can point to the training and financial benefits of national participation in a U.N. operation.

To insure that the forces actually used will meet certain minimum standards of performance, these standards must be defined and the capabilities of the donor states evaluated. Because most states have fair-to-poor military establishments, the Secretary-General will sometimes have to accept second- or third-rate forces. The larger the range of selection, the more easily the problem is solved.

Training and performance standards recommended by the staff should be communicated to all states along with the list of the types of units required. There should be visits to the potential donor's military establishment to ascertain its general and specialized capabilities. These visits should be supplemented by objective estimates of the performance of all pledged units by competent officers from other governments.

In the contract between the donor government and the Secretary-General, the quality of training expected should be specified as well as an agreed length of service for the units, preferably not less than one year. Minimum medical standards should also be specified.

4. PAY AND ALLOWANCE SCALES.   The disparity in remuneration among troops from different states serving in the Congo is inherent in the national contingent system and cannot be corrected without changing this system. There is no prospect of such a change. Giving the same basic pay to all UNF troops regardless of their national laws and customs would cause more problems than it would solve. In addition to continuing to provide equal facilities and an equal daily allowance to all troops, the Secretary-General should seek to obtain national contingents on substantially the same contractual basis. Preferably each state should provide the services of its troops without direct reimbursement for the salary or overseas allowance. It should pay its men and officers according to its national regulations. The United Nations should underwrite all other costs. In accordance with an equitable formula, donor states should receive some credit toward their peacekeeping assessment for any contribution of troops, but in no case should the extension of credit or a reimbursement permit a government to profit financially at the expense of the United Nations.

In the interests of morale in the field, the UNF command should place all contingents under the same currency regulations. Specifically, all men should operate under the same rules as to how the daily U.N. allowance should be spent and as to the amount to be converted into hard currency. The Secretary-General should attempt to dissuade donor states from giving their troops any of their basic salary or overseas allowance in the field if they are serving in an underdeveloped area. Clear-cut currency regulations strictly enforced all along the line would curb black-market activities and enhance morale.

5. OFFICER TRAINING.   A well-trained junior officer from a competent military establishment can readily adjust to

a peacekeeping mission even if the constraints are unusual, provided the mandate is reasonably clear and the force commander's orders make sense. Indoctrination courses for officers of field grade from nations with earmarked forces or capabilities would facilitate the early operations of a mission. Such courses could be given in New York or at the contemplated United Nations Training and Research Institute, or by field trips to current force operations. An officer with such training could then serve as an "expert" on peacekeeping within his national military establishment. Training costs should be largely borne by the governments furnishing the officers. Critical histories of past peacekeeping missions would also provide valuable material for introducing officers to the special problems of U.N. forces.

6. LANGUAGE. For practical reasons, reflecting both political and linguistic realities, English is recommended as the official working language of any U.N. operation involving more than a few observers. (This view was the virtually unanimous conclusion of the sixty participants of the International Conference on U.N. Security Forces held in Oslo in February 1964. Many of the participants had had responsible military or civilian positions in the Congo and Middle East operations.) All key officers assigned to a mission where English is the working language should be required to pass a test in spoken and written English.

7. MANUALS. The development of compatible doctrines, procedures, and performance standards would be facilitated by the preparation of appropriate manuals. Such manuals would have to be based on some recognized staff system, whether American, British, or French; or they should be based on a workable combination of systems. The manuals should draw upon past U.N. experience. As yet, there have been no comprehensive evaluations of peacekeeping operations involving military personnel. Most useful would be assessments of the Congo and Cyprus operations by competent military analysts

who understand the political and legal constraints of U.N. missions.

The manuals should deal with doctrine, discipline, administration, command and control, the political constraints of international peacekeeping, as well as with logistics, communications, and other customary military procedures. Since the writing of such manuals is a formidable task requiring specialized competence, their preparation should probably be assigned to qualified governments or teams of experts. For example, Canada might prepare the manual on communications, the United States the one on air transport, Britain the one on sea transportation, and Italy the one on movement control. The manuals on preventive medicine could be prepared by regional offices of the World Health Organization.

8. MULTINATIONAL UNITS.   One major lesson of the Congo experience is that small multinational units do not perform well. The desirability of one-nation working units has been fully established, the size of the unit depending upon the function. Mixed infantry battalions do not work well. Nor do small mixed movement control units or other specialized groups. Three battalions of three nationalities, each with its own national commander, can work together if the functions of each are well defined and if there is effective central command. Usually, headquarters staffs should be multinational if the force is multinational, even though this will decrease efficiency. In multinational administrative staffs it is likely that one nationality or two closely identified nationalities will tend to dominate. In the U.N. Katanga command, the Indians predominated, though Swedes and other nationalities were represented in the headquarters staff. In the various branches of the UNF command as a whole, Canadian officers tended to be placed in deputy positions.

Granted the existence of a considerable range in the sophistication of the military establishments that would have to be considered for peacekeeping operations, the ideal national contingent would be organized as a relatively self-sustaining task force. It should contain within itself most of the direct combat and service support elements required to conduct effective operations. Within the limits of political feasibility, nations which do not have this capability should usually be represented only on a nominal basis.

9. MILITARY DISCIPLINE.   The code of discipline of a military establishment is rooted deeply in its national culture. For this reason it is virtually impossible to transfer punitive sanctions to a multinational command. Nevertheless, the U.N. advisory staff could attempt to develop a minimal code of military discipline in consultation with donor states for the moral or symbolic effect it might have. At the very least, any donor state should agree in advance to deal with severe cases of indiscipline, crime, or insubordination involving one of its nationals serving in a U.N. force according to its established national code. Nevertheless, the U.N. force should retain the right to repatriate any soldier or officer found guilty of a serious violation of military discipline.

10. INTELLIGENCE AND SECURITY.   Recognizing that the gathering of intelligence is essential for the efficiency of even the simplest mission, the United Nations should recruit specialized personnel and provide adequate funds for this politically sensitive function. In New York, the military advisory staff can and should rely on cooperating governments for certain kinds of intelligence. The same is true of the U.N. commander in the field. There is no rule of thumb to indicate what categories of information the United Nations should gather on its own and what it should obtain from supporting governments. This will be governed by circumstances at the time.

Because of its multinational character, the U.N. Secretariat faces a considerably greater internal security problem than a sovereign state. While full security cannot be expected within the Organization because of the possibility of double or doubtful loyalties of some employees or co-opted personnel—a danger from which no government is completely free—a reasonable degree of administrative privacy is essential. The rudimentary security system and cipher facilities of the Secretariat should probably be strengthened.

11. PUBLIC INFORMATION.   The United Nations is not expected to engage in conventional psychological warfare, but it should be in a position to interpret the objectives of any mission to the public in the immediate area of operations as well as to the world at large. The Congo effort suffered because hostile and unfair propaganda against it found credence in a large sector of the world press. Recognizing that it should and indeed must operate in a glasshouse, not only on the East River, but in the Congo, Cyprus or elsewhere, the Secretariat should provide for qualified information specialists supported by adequate facilities.

General Observations

1. There are various perspectives from which the Congo peacekeeping effort can be evaluated. Fundamentally, however, the mission must be judged in terms of its political mandate. (This and other perspectives will be discussed in Chapter 6.) Operational efficiency may be the least important standard by which to measure the relative success or failure of the Congo experience, but it is neither irrelevant nor inconsequential. Efficiency is related not only to the material cost of an operation, but to its political cost as well. Hence, inefficiency to some extent affects adversely the capacity of any U.N. force to achieve its political objective.

2. Because of its unique international character, the performance of a multistate, nonsanctions peace force constrained by political and legal requirements, should *not* be judged by standards of efficiency appropriate to a similar operation carried out by a competent military establishment of a single

state. So judged, the general military efficiency of the UNF in the Congo would range from fair to poor. But judged by standards which take into account the inescapable constraints, the performance of the UNF was good.

3. A clear distinction should be made between those weaknesses in the Congo effort which were inherent in the fundamental nature of the internationally authorized mission and those which might have been corrected with more effective administration. Taking into account the fact that the UNF was launched without benefit of prior planning and other extenuating circumstances, there was still a certain amount of unnecessary inefficiency. Some weaknesses could have been corrected by a stronger and more efficient civilian and military administration and by a better coordination within the Secretariat, especially between the UNF command and the Field Operations Service.

4. The efficiency of the Congo operation could have been enhanced with a modest degree of prior planning consistent with the nature of nonsanctions forces and compatible with the interests of the powers involved. Among the more important measures designed to enhance readiness and operational efficiency are a small increase in the Secretary-General's military advisory staff, the earmarking by member states of units and capabilities for potential service in a U.N. force, and the preparation of operational manuals as guidelines for any future missions.

5. None of the measures intended to increase either the speed with which the Secretary-General could launch an approved mission or the efficiency with which he could carry it out will have more than a marginal effect on the probability of a mission being authorized in a given crisis. Whether or not a peacekeeping force will be authorized by the Security Council or the General Assembly is determined by the interplay of power and interest among the governments of sovereign states.

6

Appraisal and Conclusions

The United Nations cannot permanently protect the Congo, or any other country, from the internal tensions and disturbances created by its organic growth toward unity and nationhood. U THANT, JUNE 29, 1964

WALTER LIPPMANN once called the Congo peacekeeping effort "the most advanced and sophisticated experiment in international cooperation ever attempted."[1] Four years later, Arthur Krock referred to the United Nations operation as "the bloody war to suppress the establishment of Katanga as a separate state by Moise Tshombe."[2] The dramatic events that took place in the Congo between these two statements do not fully ratify Lippmann's expectations nor justify Krock's conclusion. But they do reflect the controversial character of the novel enterprise. On one fundamental point there is no disagreement—the U.N. effort was the most complex and protracted operation ever authorized, financed, and administered by an international organization. As such it merits intensive critical analysis.

Throughout the present study, fact has been combined with evaluation. This chapter is a general assessment of the entire peacekeeping effort, summarizing or supplementing what has been said before.

The several perspectives from which the pioneering operation might be evaluated can be identified by five questions:

---

[1] *Washington Post and Times Herald,* July 21, 1960.
[2] *New York Times,* Dec. 4, 1964.

171

1. Was it true to its mandate?
2. Was it efficient?
3. What effect did it have upon the Congo?
4. How did it affect the interests of other states?
5. Did it support the larger interests of international peace and security?

Before turning to these questions (each of which has been dealt with directly or indirectly in the previous chapters), it may be helpful to consider speculatively a prior question: Was there a feasible alternative to U.N. intervention in the Congo in July 1960? Was an international operation a viable option in terms of American interests?

Alternatives to U.N. Intervention

To reexamine a complex historical event like the Congo crisis of 1960 and conjecture what might have happened if different decisions had been made about the fundamental problem of outside assistance is both risky and of limited predictive and analytical value. Nevertheless, a brief retrospective assessment of the feasibility of alternative courses to U.N. intervention may throw some light on what actually happened. Theoretically, there were four possible sources of outside assistance: Belgium, some African states, the Soviet Union, and the United States. Each will be considered in turn after dealing with the alternative of no outside assistance at all.

To sharpen the focus of this hypothetical exercise, the analysis will be made from the perspective of America's interest in maintaining stability in central Africa. Specifically, U.S. policy was directed toward the creation of a united and stable Congo with a moderate government capable of having mutually beneficial diplomatic and economic relations with the West. It will be assumed without argument that Washington's objectives were not incompatible with long-range African interests or the larger interests of international peace.

Given the desperate situation occasioned by the abrupt departure of Belgian authority, outside intervention—invited or uninvited—was inevitable. As noted in Chapter 1, when the Congolese government requested the U.S. ambassador for American military assistance, the ambassador advised it to address its request to the Secretary-General. This advice, subsequently ratified by Secretary of State Herter and President Eisenhower, was followed by Prime Minister Lumumba and President Kasavubu. Had the Congolese government tried without assistance to deal with the army mutinies, certainly the Belgians would have intervened to save their nationals living there. This intervention would doubtless have been the pretext for Soviet intervention directly or through the cooperation of states such as the United Arab Republic, Ghana, or Guinea. The fact that certain states did intervene openly or covertly in Congolese affairs after the United Nations had been given the exclusive responsibility for restoring order indicates that the absence of invited assistance would probably have compounded the chaos and have led to the balkanization of the Congo.

Since outside assistance was needed, the new government theoretically could have turned to Belgium, some African states, or the Soviet Union.

1. Belgium was probably physically capable of restoring and maintaining order after the army mutinies, if other powers such as the Soviet Union had remained aloof. This is a big "if." Under the unratified Treaty of Friendship with Leopoldville, Belgium held its military bases at Kamina and Kitona. Brussels offered to make troops from these bases available to restore order. When the offer was rejected by Lumumba, the Belgians dispatched paratroopers to the Congo and deployed them against his wishes, which drew the charge of "aggression" from the Congolese government. After this development there was little chance that Belgian assistance would be requested, certainly not as long as Lumumba remained in office.

If the increasingly anti-Western and pro-Communist Lumumba had not been Prime Minister, it is quite possible that President Kasavubu and other moderate Congolese leaders would have invited the Belgian troops to restore order after the original mutiny—a move that would have foreshadowed what actually occurred in January 1964, when the governments of the three new East African states called upon Britain, the former metropolitan power, to put down troop mutinies. The plausibility of this hypothesis is buttressed by the fact that the Kasavubu-Adoula government turned increasingly to the Belgians for assistance in the security field. But with Lumumba as Prime Minister, the speed of unravelling events, and panic on the part of the Belgians, invited Belgian assistance was not a feasible alternative in 1960. In 1963, it did become feasible, and more than a year before the UNF left the Congo, the Adoula government urgently requested Belgian military assistance. This request was supported by Washington.

2. At no point was there any real chance for the Leopoldville government to secure reliable military assistance from any African state or combination of states. No African government politically acceptable to Lumumba had the military, logistical, or financial capability to send more than a token force to the Congo. Further, there was no existing African regional organization capable of authorizing, creating, and dispatching a peacekeeping force composed of African units. Even if a coalition of African states could have raised a force, it is doubtful that these states could have agreed politically on the function of the force within the Congo.

Leopoldville would hardly have invited a single state, like the United Arab Republic, Ghana, or Guinea, to send even a token force, because the Congolese government had no assurance that such a force would refrain from illegal and irresponsible behavior. It was believed that some of the troops of Ghana and Guinea serving in the UNF were involved in subversive activities against the Central Government, possibly in behalf of the Soviet bloc. These activities were presumed to have included an attempt to assassinate high Congolese officials, the chief of staff of the Congolese army.[3]

3. With a legitimate invitation to send military assistance,

3 See page 58.

the Soviet Union could have flown in troops, if Moscow could have secured the necessary landing, overflight, and refueling rights from a number of states en route. Given the opposition of Washington, London, and other governments to the establishment of a Soviet military presence in Central Africa, the granting of such rights was unlikely. Had these political obstacles been overcome, and had the Soviet Union dispatched a force, it is possible that it could have restored order. But the United States would hardly have looked with equanimity upon even a temporary Russian military-political presence in the Congo.

4. Perhaps the least implausible alternative to U.N. intervention in July 1960, would have been American assistance. Washington was the only capital to receive an invitation to help that was militarily capable of restoring order, though American assistance might have provoked new disorders. A series of interrelated considerations led the U.S. government to reject direct aid and to advise the Congolese government to turn to the United Nations. In the first place, the situation was very confused and it was not clear exactly what functions should be performed by outside assistance. In the beginning, the problem was to suppress the army mutinies in several camps, a relatively simple task which could probably have been accomplished quickly by a well-organized token force of European troops of any nationality. But with the panic of the Belgians, the deployment of Belgian paratroopers, and the secession of Katanga, the situation soon escalated into a problem of different dimensions.

In view of this confusion and Washington's general disposition to regard aid to Central African states as primarily the responsibility of former metropoles, the political risks of direct U.S. involvement seemed greater than the political risks of the slower and operationally less efficient U.N. approach. As a vocal proponent of decolonization in Africa, the State Department wanted to avoid the charges of neocolonialism that certainly would have greeted direct American aid. Further, Washington did not want to provide a pretext for more substantial Soviet intervention in behalf of Lumumba or risk any big-power confrontation which might have resulted from such intervention. The U.S. government also wished to avoid being placed in an embarrassing position between the expectations of Congolese and other neutralist leaders on the one hand and its responsibilities to Belgium and other NATO allies on the other. With little debate or dissent within the government (there was no time for lengthy deliberation), Washington quickly concluded that the political risks would be minimized and its interests would be better served if American aid to the Congo were channeled through the United Nations.

Given the circumstances, the U.S. decision to use the United Nations was inevitable. As it turned out, American objectives were well served by the U.N. peacekeeping mission, though it must be said that U.S. participation in the effort was not without risks and problems. The U.N. presence did not wholly shield the United States from charges of neocolonialism; UNF troops were called "American mercenaries" and worse. Nor did it prevent the unilateral intervention of the Soviet Union, or China, though it did limit the character of such intervention. The United Nations was unable to make any progress toward the creation of a disciplined and responsible Congolese army, with the result that the United States and Belgium, at the request of Leopoldville, launched bilateral military assistance programs in 1963, more than a year before the UNF quit the Congo.

While the U.N. operation did not prevent a political confrontation between the United States and the Communist bloc, it did impose legal and moral constraints on the situation which lent support to the forces working for a united Congo and a moderate government. Conversely, the U.N. presence on balance reinforced those elements inside and outside the Congo which sought to replace Lumumba and to frustrate Soviet ambitions in Central Africa.

This leads to the evaluation of the operation as a whole from the different perspectives identified by the five questions noted above.

1. Was the Operation True to Its Mandate?

According to the various Security Council resolutions the purposes of the peacekeeping effort, to be pursued in cooperation with the Congolese government, were as follows:

- Restore and maintain law and order.
- Protect life and property throughout the country.
- Transform the Congolese army into a reliable instrument of internal security.
- Restore and maintain the territorial integrity of the Congo.
- Prevent civil war and pacify tribal conflict.
- Protect the Congo from external interference in its affairs, particularly through the elimination of foreign mercenaries hired by secessionist Katanga.

The United Nations was expressly forbidden to take sides in the internal struggle. The record indicates that neither Hammarskjold nor Thant departed from the pursuit of these broad objectives in spite of constant efforts by factions within the Congo and outside powers to use the UNF for their parochial purposes. Nevertheless, both Secretaries-General and their chief aides in the Congo were frequently assailed for taking sides in the internal struggles. Dayal, for example, was accused of supporting Lumumba's cause after Lumumba was dismissed by Kasavubu. Though there is some basis for this accusation, it must be remembered that the Congo during the period of the political vacuum was a legal and political snake pit and it was impossible for any high Secretariat official on the scene to be regarded as fair by conflicting parties. As noted in Chapter 2, the net impact of the U.N. presence, whether intended or not, was support for a moderate government representing all major factions against the claims of Lumumba on the one hand and the aspirations of Tshombe on the other.

In addition to the constraints of noninterference and the necessity for the consent of the host government for any significant action, UNF troops were restricted by limitations on the use of force specified by the Security Council. Though the original restriction of military force to self-defense was broadened to permit force to prevent civil war and apprehend foreign mercenaries, the UNF operated under constraints more severe than those of a conventional army or even of a domestic police force. The United Nations was never given the authority to use force to end the secession of Katanga.

With the exception of O'Brien's avowed attempt to end Katangan secession, in which UNF troops used military force, the operation never exceeded its legal authority as defined by the Council. As a matter of fact, the Secretary-General did not use all the authority he had because of the frequent lack of consent of the Central Government, inadequate military strength, partial opposition by some great powers, and his strong desire to avoid the use of force except as a last resort. For these and other reasons the UNF's right to "freedom of movement" was exercised fully only in Round Three, which succeeded in ending Katangan secession.

2. Was the Operation Efficient?

Operational efficiency may be the least important standard by which to judge an international peacekeeping effort, but factors of speed, economy, and quality are not irrelevant. As noted in Chapter 5, the efficiency of the Congo operation should not be measured by standards appropriate to a similar mission carried out by a competent military establishment of a single state. It should be measured by standards which take into account its political mandate, the legal constraints, and the multinational character of the Force. So judged, the efficiency of the U.N. effort was good. This does not mean it could not have been improved by better administration, or that future operations might not benefit by a modest degree of prior planning. The earmarking of capabilities by member states and a slight strengthening of the U.N. military advisory staff would enhance the speed and efficiency of any future mission, but would not necessarily increase the number of such missions.

3. What Was the Effect of the Operation Upon the Congo?

The fundamental basis for judging the relative success or failure of the Congo effort is its impact upon the Congo and the larger interests of peace and security. As noted in Chapter 4, the UNF was only one of many actors in the unfolding drama and can, therefore, neither be blamed for all that went wrong nor be given full credit for any positive steps toward greater law and order. Though it is impossible to measure the effect of the various factors on the Congo situation, this study concludes that insofar as the UNF had an influence it was on the side of supporting a united Congo with a moderate and representative constitutional government.

The United Nations frustrated efforts by the Soviet Union to support the Stanleyville regime in 1960 when it closed the airports to Soviet and all but U.N. aircraft. The UNF helped to end Katangan secession, thus eliminating one major challenge to the territorial integrity of the Congo. It did nothing, however, about the equally serious challenge to the authority of the Central Government posed by the Communist-supported rebel movements of 1964.

The UNF helped to maintain order and to deter tribal strife in areas where its units were deployed. It helped to protect life and property. It protected U.N. personnel engaged in essential civilian services.

All these accomplishments were in harmony with the Council mandate.

But the United Nations did not succeed in what was perhaps its most important assignment—the training and reorganization of the Congolese army. As a result, the army was almost as irresponsible and unreliable after four years of peacekeeping as it was when the first U.N. soldier set foot on Congolese soil. What improvement there may have been in the army was due to the bilateral efforts of the United States, Belgium, and Israel. The responsibility for this major failure must be shared by the Congolese government and the United Nations.

4. How Did the Operation Affect the Interests of Other States?

The interests of those states seeking stability in Central Africa and a united Congo under a moderate government were served by the U.N. effort. The interests of those states to isolate Katanga, to balkanize the Congo, or to install an extreme nationalist or pro-Communist regime in Leopoldville were frustrated. The governments seeking stability included the United States, Britain, Belgium, France, and most other Western states, as well as moderate neutralist states such as Tunisia, Ethiopia, Nigeria, and India. It must be said, however, that London, Brussels, and Paris were prepared to rely more on Tshombe for stability than was Washington. The governments supporting an extreme nationalist or pro-Communist regime included Russia, China, the smaller Communist states, as well as Ghana, Guinea, the United Arab Republic, and Algeria. A few governments, like those of South Africa, the Federation of Rhodesia and Nyasaland, and Portugal, seemed to support Katangan independence, though none ever accorded diplomatic recognition to Tshombe's "independent state." This rough characterization of interests must be read in light of the occasional lapses into inconsistency on the part of the statesmen involved.

Of the great powers, the United States was the chief beneficiary of the U.N. mission whose net effect was to support a moderate Congo government capable of sustaining mutually beneficial relations with the West. This was true, not because the United Nations was an instrument of the State Department, as the Soviet Union has repeatedly charged, but because there was a high degree of concurrence between U.S. objectives and the objectives of the Security Council. Conversely, the Soviet Union was the chief loser. Since the U.N. operation did not make the Congo safe for Lumumba and the Russians, it was regarded as a betrayal of Soviet interests in the heart of Africa.

Though British and French interests in stability in Africa appear to have been served by the UNF, both these governments regarded the mission as having established a dangerous precedent. France opposed the mission in principle, while Britain's opposition was confined to the use of a military force to end Katangan secession, which London insisted was an illegal and unwise penetration of the United Nations into the internal affairs of a sovereign state.

5. *Were the Larger Interests of Peace Served by the Operation?*

The Congo peacekeeping effort was a novel, controversial, and a less-than-efficient enterprise. It sometimes fumbled. It made many small mistakes. It was assailed on all sides. It precipitated a financial crisis for the United Nations. But in the final analysis, the U.N. Force must be judged by its contribution to international stability, regardless of what other interests it might have served. So judged, the mission succeeded. It contributed to peace and security in Central Africa and in the wider world.

As the largest and most complex internationally authorized and administered operation in history, the Congo peacekeeping effort is rich in lessons and warnings for the future.

Appendixes

APPENDIX **A**

Selected Articles
from the United Nations Charter

ARTICLE 2

4. All Members shall refrain in their international relations from the threat or use of force against the territorial integrity or political independence of any state, or in any other manner inconsistent with the Purposes of the United Nations.

5. All Members shall give the United Nations every assistance in any action it takes in accordance with the present Charter, and shall refrain from giving assistance to any state against which the United Nations is taking preventive or enforcement action.

7. Nothing contained in the present Charter shall authorize the United Nations to intervene in matters which are essentially within the domestic jurisdiction of any state or shall require the Members to submit such matters to settlement under the present Charter; but this principle shall not prejudice the application of enforcement measures under Chapter VII.

ARTICLE 22

The General Assembly may establish such subsidiary organs as it deems necessary for the performance of its functions.

ARTICLE 25

The Members of the United Nations agree to accept and carry out the decisions of the Security Council in accordance with the present Charter.

ARTICLE 27

1. Each member of the Security Council shall have one vote.

2. Decisions of the Security Council on procedural matters shall be made by an affirmative vote of seven members.

3. Decisions of the Security Council on all other matters shall be made by an affirmative vote of seven members including the

concurring votes of the permanent members; provided that, in decisions under Chapter VI, and under paragraph 3 of Article 52, a party to a dispute shall abstain from voting.

ARTICLE 29

The Security Council may establish such subsidiary organs as it deems necessary for the performance of its functions.

Chapter VI: Pacific Settlement of Disputes

ARTICLE 34

The Security Council may investigate any dispute, or any situation which might lead to international friction or give rise to a dispute, in order to determine whether the continuance of the dispute or situation is likely to endanger the maintenance of international peace and security.

ARTICLE 36

1. The Security Council may, at any stage of a dispute of the nature referred to in Article 33 or of a situation of like nature, recommend appropriate procedures or methods of adjustment.

ARTICLE 37

2. If the Security Council deems that the continuance of the dispute is in fact likely to endanger the maintenance of international peace and security, it shall decide whether to take action under Article 36 or to recommend such terms of settlement as it may consider appropriate.

Chapter VII: Action With Respect to Threats to the Peace, Breaches of the Peace, and Acts of Aggression

ARTICLE 39

The Security Council shall determine the existence of any threat to the peace, breach of the peace, or act of aggression and shall make recommendations, or decide what measures shall be taken in accordance with Articles 41 and 42, to maintain or restore international peace and security.

ARTICLE 40

In order to prevent an aggravation of the situation, the Security Council may, before making the recommendations or deciding upon the measures provided for in Article 39, call upon the parties concerned to comply with such provisional measures as it deems necessary or desirable. Such provisional measures shall be without prejudice to the rights, claims, or position of the parties concerned.

The Security Council shall duly take account of failure to comply with such provisional measures.

ARTICLE 41

The Security Council may decide what measures not involving the use of armed force are to be employed to give effect to its decisions, and it may call upon the Members of the United Nations to apply such measures. These may include complete or partial interruption of economic relations and of rail, sea, air, postal, telegraphic, radio, and other means of communication, and the severance of diplomatic relations.

ARTICLE 42

Should the Security Council consider that measures provided for in Article 41 would be inadequate or have proved to be inadequate, it may take such action by air, sea, or land forces as may be necessary to maintain or restore international peace and security. Such action may include demonstrations, blockade, and other operations by air, sea, or land forces of Members of the United Nations.

ARTICLE 43

1. All Members of the United Nations, in order to contribute to the maintenance of international peace and security, undertake to make available to the Security Council, on its call and in accordance with a special agreement or agreements, armed forces, assistance, and facilities, including rights of passage, necessary for the purpose of maintaining international peace and security.

2. Such agreement or agreements shall govern the numbers and types of forces, their degree of readiness and general location, and the nature of the facilities and assistance to be provided.

3. The agreement or agreements shall be negotiated as soon as possible on the initiative of the Security Council. They shall be concluded between the Security Council and Members or between the Security Council and groups of Members and shall be subject to ratification by the signatory states in accordance with their respective constitutional processes.

ARTICLE 44

When the Security Council has decided to use force it shall, before calling upon a Member not represented on it to provide armed forces in fulfillment of the obligations assumed under Article 43, invite that Member, if the Member so desires, to participate in the decisions of the Security Council concerning the employment of contingents of that Member's armed forces.

ARTICLE 45

In order to enable the United Nations to take urgent military measures, Members shall hold immediately available national air-force contingents for combined international enforcement action. The strength and degree of readiness of these contingents and plans for their combined action shall be determined, within the limits laid down in the special agreement or agreements referred to in Article 43, by the Security Council with the assistance of the Military Staff Committee.

ARTICLE 46

Plans for the application of armed force shall be made by the Security Council with the assistance of the Military Staff Committee.

ARTICLE 47

1. There shall be established a Military Staff Committee to advise and assist the Security Council on all questions relating to the Security Council's military requirements for the maintenance of international peace and security, the employment and command of forces placed at its disposal, the regulation of armaments, and possible disarmament.

2. The Military Staff Committee shall consist of the Chiefs of Staff of the permanent members of the Security Council or their representatives. Any Member of the United Nations not permanently represented on the Committee shall be invited by the Committee to be associated with it when the efficient discharge of the Committee's responsibilities requires the participation of that Member in its work.

3. The Military Staff Committee shall be responsible under the Security Council for the strategic direction of any armed forces placed at the disposal of the Security Council. Questions relating to the command of such forces shall be worked out subsequently.

4. The Military Staff Committee, with the authorization of the Security Council and after consultation with appropriate regional agencies, may establish regional subcommittees.

ARTICLE 48

1. The action required to carry out the decisions of the Security Council for the maintenance of international peace and security shall be taken by all the Members of the United Nations or by some of them, as the Security Council may determine.

2. Such decisions shall be carried out by the Members of the

United Nations directly and through their action in the appropriate international agencies of which they are members.

ARTICLE 49

The Members of the United Nations shall join in affording mutual assistance in carrying out the measures decided upon by the Security Council.

ARTICLE 50

If preventive or enforcement measures against any state are taken by the Security Council, any other state, whether a Member of the United Nations or not, which finds itself confronted with special economic problems arising from the carrying out of those measures shall have the right to consult the Security Council with regard to a solution of those problems.

ARTICLE 51

Nothing in the present Charter shall impair the inherent right of individual or collective self-defense if an armed attack occurs against a Member of the United Nations, until the Security Council has taken measures necessary to maintain international peace and security. Measures taken by Members in the exercise of this right of self-defense shall be immediately reported to the Security Council and shall not in any way affect the authority and responsibility of the Security Council under the present Charter to take at any time such action as it deems necessary in order to maintain or restore international peace and security.

ARTICLE 99

The Secretary-General may bring to the attention of the Security Council any matter which in his opinion may threaten the maintenance of international peace and security.

APPENDIX B

Security Council and General Assembly
Resolutions on the Congo

1. SECURITY COUNCIL, JULY 14, 1960

[Resolution S/4387 was adopted by 8 votes—Argentina, Ceylon, Ecuador, Italy, Poland, Tunisia, the Soviet Union, and the United States—to 0. There were 3 abstentions—China, France, and the United Kingdom.]

Considering the report of the Secretary-General on a request for United Nations action in relation to the Republic of the Congo,

Considering the request for military assistance addressed to the Secretary-General by the President and the Prime Minister of the Republic of the Congo (document S/4382),

1. *Calls upon* the Government of Belgium to withdraw their troops from the territory of the Republic of the Congo;

2. *Decides* to authorize the Secretary-General to take the necessary steps, in consultation with the Government of the Republic of the Congo, to provide the Government with such military assistance as may be necessary, until, through the efforts of the Congolese Government with the technical assistance of the United Nations, the national security forces may be able, in the opinion of the Government, to meet fully their tasks;

3. *Requests* the Secretary-General to report to the Security Council as appropriate.

2. SECURITY COUNCIL, JULY 22, 1960

[Resolution S/4405 was adopted unanimously.]

Having considered the first report by the Secretary-General on the implementation of Security Council resolution S/4387 of 14 July 1960 (document S/4389),

Appreciating the work of the Secretary-General and the support so readily and so speedily given to him by all Member States invited by him to give assistance,

Noting that as stated by the Secretary-General the arrival of the troops of the United Nations force in Leopoldville has already had a salutary effect,

Recognizing that an urgent need still exists to continue and to increase such efforts,

Considering that the complete restoration of law and order in the Republic of the Congo would effectively contribute to the maintenance of international peace and security,

Recognizing that the Security Council recommended the admission of the Republic of the Congo to membership in the United Nations as a unit,

1. *Calls upon* the Government of Belgium to implement speedily the Security Council resolution of 14 July 1960, on the withdrawal of their troops, and *authorizes* the Secretary-General to take all necessary action to this effect;

2. *Requests* all States to refrain from any action which might tend to impede the restoration of law and order and the exercise by the Government of the Congo of its authority and also to refrain from any action which might undermine the territorial integrity and the political independence of the Republic of the Congo;

3. *Commends* the Secretary-General for the prompt action he has taken to carry out resolution S/4387 of the Security Council and his first report;

4. *Invites* the specialized agencies of the United Nations to render to the Secretary-General such assistance as he may require;

5. *Requests* the Secretary-General to report further to the Security Council as appropriate.

3. SECURITY COUNCIL, AUGUST 9, 1960

[Resolution S/4426 was adopted by 9 votes to 0. There were 2 abstentions—France and Italy.]

Recalling its resolution of 22 July 1960 (S/4405) *inter alia,* calling upon the Government of Belgium to implement speedily the Security Council resolution of 14 July (S/4387) on the withdrawal of their troops, and authorizing the Secretary-General to take all necessary action to this effect,

Having noted the second report by the Secretary-General on the implementation of the aforesaid two resolutions and his statement before the Council,

Having considered the statements made by the representatives of Belgium and the Republic of the Congo to this Council at this meeting,

Noting with satisfaction the progress made by the United Nations in carrying out the Security Council resolution in respect of the territory of the Republic of the Congo other than the Province of Katanga,

Noting however that the United Nations had been prevented from implementing the aforesaid resolutions in the Province of Katanga although it was ready, and in fact attempted, to do so,

Recognizing that the withdrawal of Belgian troops from the Province of Katanga will be a positive contribution to and essential for the proper implementation of the Security Council resolutions,

1. *Confirms* the authority given to the Secretary-General by the Security Council resolutions of 14 July and 22 July 1960 and *requests* him to continue to carry out the responsibility placed on him thereby;

2. *Calls upon* the Government of Belgium to withdraw immediately its troops from the Province of Katanga under speedy modalities determined by the Secretary-General and to assist in every possible way the implementation of the Council's resolutions;

3. *Declares* that the entry of the United Nations force into the Province of Katanga is necessary for the full implementation of this resolution;

4. *Reaffirms* that the United Nations force in the Congo will not be a party to or in any way intervene in or be used to influence the outcome of any internal conflict, constitutional or otherwise;

5. *Calls upon* all Member States, in accordance with Articles 25 and 49 of the Charter, to accept and carry out the decisions of the Security Council and to afford mutual assistance in carrying out measures decided upon by the Security Council;

6. *Requests* the Secretary-General to implement this resolution and to report further to the Security Council as appropriate.

4. GENERAL ASSEMBLY, SEPTEMBER 20, 1960

[Resolution A/4510 was adopted by 70 votes to 0. There were 11 abstentions—Albania, Bulgaria, Byelorussia, Czechoslovakia, France, Hungary, Poland, Romania, the Ukraine, Union of South Africa and the Soviet Union. Bolivia was absent.]

Having considered the situation in the Republic of the Congo,

Taking note of the resolutions of 14 and 22 July and of 9 August 1960 of the Security Council,

Taking into account the unsatisfactory economic and political conditions that continue in the Republic of the Congo,

Considering that, with a view to preserving the unity, territorial integrity and political independence of the Congo, to protecting and advancing the welfare of its people, and to safeguarding international peace, it is essential for the United Nations to continue to assist the Central Government of the Congo,

1. *Fully supports* the resolutions of 14 and 22 July and of 9 August of the Security Council;

2. *Requests* the Secretary-General to continue to take vigorous action in accordance with the terms of the aforesaid resolutions and to assist the Central Government of the Congo in the restoration and maintenance of law and order throughout the territory of the Republic of the Congo and to safeguard its unity, territorial integrity and political independence in the interests of international peace and security;

3. *Appeals* to all Congolese within the Republic of the Congo to seek a speedy solution by peaceful means of all their internal conflicts for the unity and integrity of the Congo, with the assistance, as appropriate, of Asian and African representatives appointed by the Advisory Committee on the Congo, in consultation with the Secretary-General, for the purpose of conciliation;

4. *Appeals* to all Member Governments for urgent voluntary contributions to a United Nations Fund for the Congo to be used under United Nations control and in consultation with the Central Government for the purpose of rendering the fullest possible assistance to achieve the objective mentioned in the preamble;

5. *Requests*

(a) All States to refrain from any action which might tend to impede the restoration of law and order and the exercise by the Government of the Congo of its authority and also to refrain from any action which might undermine the unity, territorial integrity and political independence of the Republic of the Congo;

(b) All Member States, in accordance with Articles 25 and 49 of the Charter, to accept and carry out the decisions of the Security Council and to afford mutual assistance in carrying out measures decided upon by the Security Council;

6. Without prejudice to the sovereign rights of the Republic of the Congo, *calls upon* all States to refrain from the direct and indirect provision of arms or other material of war and military personnel and other assistance for military purposes in the Congo during the temporary period of military assistance through the United Nations, except upon the request of the United Nations through the Secretary-General for carrying out the purposes of this resolution and of the resolutions of 14 and 22 July and of 9 August 1960 of the Security Council.

5. SECURITY COUNCIL, FEBRUARY 21, 1961

[Resolution S/4741 was adopted by 9 votes to 0. There were 2 abstentions—France and the Soviet Union.]

A

Having considered the situation in the Congo,

Having learned with deep regret the announcement of the killing of the Congolese leaders, Mr. Patrice Lumumba, Mr. Maurice Mpolo and Mr. Joseph Okito,

Deeply concerned at the grave repercussions of these crimes and the danger of wide-spread civil war and bloodshed in the Congo and the threat to international peace and security,

Noting the Report of the Secretary-General's Special Representative (S/4691) dated 12 February 1961 bringing to light the development of a serious civil war situation and preparations therefor,

1. *Urges* that the United Nations take immediately all appropriate measures to prevent the occurrence of civil war in the Congo, including arrangements for cease-fires, the halting of all military operations, the prevention of clashes, and the use of force, if necessary, in the last resort;

2. *Urges* that measures be taken for the immediate withdrawal and evacuation from the Congo of all Belgian and other foreign military and para-military personnel and political advisers not under the United Nations Command, and mercenaries;

3. *Calls* upon all States to take immediate and energetic measures to prevent the departure of such personnel for the Congo from their territories, and for the denial of transit and other facilities to them;

4. *Decides* that an immediate and impartial investigation be held in order to ascertain the circumstances of the death of Mr. Lumumba and his colleagues and that the perpetrators of these crimes be punished;

5. *Reaffirms* the Security Council resolutions of 14 July, 22 July, and 9 August 1960 and the General Assembly resolution 1474 (ES-IV) of 20 September 1960 and reminds all States of their obligation under these resolutions.

B

The Security Council,

Gravely concerned at the continuing deterioration in the Congo, and the prevalence of conditions which seriously imperil peace and order, and the unity and territorial integrity of the Congo, and threaten international peace and security,

Noting with deep regret and concern the systematic violations of human rights and fundamental freedoms and the general absence of rule of law in the Congo,

Recognizing the imperative necessity of the restoration of parliamentary institutions in the Congo in accordance with the fundamental law of the country, so that the will of the people should be reflected through the freely elected Parliament,

Convinced that the solution of the problem of the Congo lies in the hands of the Congolese people themselves without any interference from outside and that there can be no solution without conciliation,

Convinced further that the imposition of any solution, including the formation of any government not based on genuine conciliation would, far from settling any issues, greatly enhance the dangers of conflict within the Congo and threat to international peace and security,

1. *Urges* the convening of the Parliament and the taking of necessary protective measures in that connection;

2. *Urges* that Congolese armed units and personnel should be reorganized and brought under discipline and control, and arrangements be made on impartial and equitable bases to that end and with a view to the elimination of any possibility of interference by such units and personnel in the political life of the Congo;

3. *Calls upon* all States to extend their full co-operation and assistance and take such measures as may be necessary on their part, for the implementation of this resolution.

6. SECURITY COUNCIL, NOVEMBER 24, 1961

[Resolution S/5002 was adopted by 9 votes to 0. There were 2 abstentions—France and the United Kingdom.]

Recalling its resolutions S/4387, S/4405, S/4426 and S/4741,

Recalling further General Assembly resolutions 1474 (ES-IV), 1592 (XV), 1599 (XV), 1600 (XV) and 1601 (XV),

Reaffirming the policies and purposes of the United Nations with respect to the Congo (Leopoldville) as set out in the aforesaid resolutions, namely:

(a) To maintain the territorial integrity and the political independence of the Republic of the Congo;

(b) To assist the Central Government of the Congo in the restoration and maintenance of law and order;

(c) To prevent the occurrence of civil war in the Congo;

(d) To secure the immediate withdrawal and evacuation from the Congo of all foreign military, para-military and advisory personnel not under the United Nations Command, and all mercenaries; and

(e) To render technical assistance;

Welcoming the restoration of the national Parliament of the Congo in accordance with the *Loi fondamentale* and the consequent formation of a Central Government on 2 August 1961,

Deploring all armed action in opposition to the authority of the Government of the Republic of the Congo, specifically secessionist activities and armed action now being carried on by the Provincial Administration of Katanga with the aid of external resources and foreign mercenaries, and *completely rejecting* the claim that Katanga is a "sovereign independent nation,"

Noting with deep regret the recent and past actions of violence against United Nations personnel,

Recognizing the Government of the Republic of the Congo as exclusively responsible for the conduct of the external affairs of the Congo,

Bearing in mind the imperative necessity of speedy and effective action to implement fully the policies and purposes of the United Nations in the Congo to end the unfortunate plight of the Congolese people, necessary both in the interests of world peace and international cooperation, and stability and progress of Africa as a whole,

1. *Strongly deprecates* the secessionist activities illegally carried out by the provincial administration of Katanga, with the aid of external resources and manned by foreign mercenaries;

2. *Further deprecates* the armed action against United Nations forces and personnel in the pursuit of such activities;

3. *Insists* that such activities shall cease forthwith, and *calls upon* all concerned to desist therefrom;

4. *Authorizes* the Secretary-General to take vigorous action, including the use of a requisite measure of force, if necessary, for the immediate apprehension, detention pending legal action and/or deportation of all foreign military and para-military personnel and political advisers not under the United Nations Command, and mercenaries as laid down in paragraph A-2 of the Security Council resolution of 21 February 1961;

5. *Further requests* the Secretary-General to take all necessary measures to prevent the entry or return of such elements under whatever guise and also of arms, equipment or other material in support of such activities;

6. *Requests* all States to refrain from the supply of arms, equipment or other material which could be used for warlike purposes, and to take the necessary measures to prevent their nationals from doing the same, and also to deny transportation and transit facilities for such supplies across their territories, except in accordance with the decisions, policies and purposes of the United Nations;

7. *Calls upon* all Member States to refrain from promoting, condoning, or giving support by acts of omission or commission, directly or indirectly, to activities against the United Nations often resulting in armed hostilities against the United Nations forces and personnel;

8. *Declares* that all secessionist activities against the Republic of the Congo are contrary to the *Loi fondamentale* and Security Council decisions and specifically *demands* that such activities which are now taking place in Katanga shall cease forthwith;

9. *Declares* full and firm support for the Central Government of the Congo, and the determination to assist that Government in accordance with the decision of the United Nations to maintain law and order and

national integrity, to provide technical assistance and to implement those decisions;

10. *Urges* all Member States to lend their support, according to their national procedures, to the Central Government of the Republic of the Congo, in conformity with the Charter and the decisions of the United Nations;

11. *Requests* all Member States to refrain from any action which may directly or indirectly impede the policies and purposes of the United Nations in the Congo and is contrary to its decisions and the general purpose of the Charter.

Agreement Between the United Nations and the Congolese Government

Note: This "basic agreement" between Mr. Hammarskjold and the Congo was initialled on July 29, 1960. It was circulated as document S/4389/Add. 5.

1. The Government of the Republic of the Congo states that, in the exercise of its sovereign rights with respect to any question concerning the presence and functioning of the United Nations Force in the Congo, it will be guided, in good faith, by the fact that it has requested military assistance from the United Nations and by its acceptance of the resolutions of the Security Council of 14 and 22 July 1960; it likewise states that it will ensure the freedom of movement of the Force in the interior of the country and will accord the requisite privileges and immunities to all personnel associated with the activities of the Force.

2. The United Nations takes note of this statement of the Government of the Republic of the Congo and states that, with regard to the activities of the United Nations Force in the Congo, it will be guided, in good faith, by the task assigned to the Force in the aforementioned resolutions; in particular the United Nations reaffirms, considering it to be in accordance with the wishes of the Government of the Republic of the Congo, that it is prepared to maintain the United Nations Force in the Congo until such time as it deems the latter's task to have been fully accomplished.

3. The Government of the Republic of the Congo and the Secretary-General state their intention to proceed immediately, in the light of paragraphs 1 and 2 above, to explore jointly specific aspects of the functioning of the United Nations Force in the Congo, notably with respect to its deployment, the question of its lines of communication and supply, its lodging and its provisioning; the Government of the Republic of the Congo, confirming its intention to facilitate the functioning of the United Nations Force in the Congo, and the United Nations have agreed to work together to hasten the implementation of the guiding principles laid down in consequence of the work of joint exploration on the basis of the resolutions of the Security Council.

4. The foregoing provisions shall likewise be applicable, as appropriate, to the non-military aspects of the United Nations operation in the Congo.

Treaty of Friendship Between
Belgium and the Congo

Note: This unofficial translation of the Treaty is reprinted from the *Staff Memorandum on the Republic of the Congo,* Committee on Foreign Affairs, House of Representatives, Washington, D.C., August 24, 1960, page 58.

The High Contracting Parties, considering that it is in their common interest to maintain between themselves ties of friendship and solidarity, in respect to the sovereignty of each of the two independent States, have drawn up the following provisions:

1. The High Contracting Parties are concluding between themselves a general treaty of friendship, assistance and technical cooperation. They will entertain a mutual collaboration on a basis of equality and will consult each other on all matters of common interest.

2. The Belgian Government will put at the disposal of and under the authority of the Congolese Government, under the conditions decreed in the common accord, personnel in the administrative, judiciary, military, cultural, and scientific fields and in the field of education.

3. Assistance and cooperation in the social, economic and financial fields will be determined by agreements put forth commonly.

4. The provisions foreseen in Articles 2 and 3 will be based on the resolutions and work of the Round Table and the Economic and Social Conferences.

5. To assure the representation of the Congo and the protection of the Congo's aims and interests abroad, the Belgian Government will collaborate with the Congolese Government, notably: in assuming Congo representation wherever the Congolese Government desires it; by putting at the disposition of the Congo, to a degree desired by the Congolese Government, personnel of the Belgian Ministry of Foreign Affairs.

6. All military intervention by Belgian forces stationed in Congo bases can take place only on the express command of the Congolese Minister of National Defense. Agreements to be made later will set the measures under which the Belgian military bases in the Congo will revert to the Congo and will set forward in detail the forms of cooperation desired by the two governments.

7. The Governments of Belgium and of the Congo will proceed to

exchange diplomatic missions which apart from the powers, privileges and immunities accorded to all embassies will be beneficiaries of a special status.

The chiefs of these missions will be able to be present at Committee of Ministers meetings as provided in the protocol of Article 9. They will equally be able, when invited, to be present at the Committee of Ministers meetings of the other Contracting Party.

Because of these prerogatives they will enjoy a special protocol position.

The Congo will be able to be represented in Belgium by a Minister, member of the Government of the Republic, in view of the importance of the problems which must be worked out between the two States.

For the realization of the program of assistance and cooperation provided for in Articles 2, 3, 5 and 6 of the present treaty, the Belgian diplomatic representation in the Congo will include a technical assistance mission.

8. As pertains to relations in the fields of commerce, maritime transportation and public adjudications, the High Contracting Parties commit themselves to grant reciprocally a treatment which is as favorable as that which they would grant to another state because of a special agreement and not to give any other state treatment which is more favorable than that agreed between the two.

9. To assure full effectiveness of the cooperation provided for in the first Article, the Governments of the High Contracting Parties and their representatives will proceed to a regular exchange of views.

10. Litigation resulting from the application of the present treaty which cannot be decided notably by application of Article 9 will be resolved according to an arbitration procedure established by a separate convention.

11. Separate conventions will set forward in detail the modalities of application of the clauses set forth in Articles 2, 3, 5, 6, 7, 8, 9, and 10.

12. The treaty is concluded for an indefinite period. Either of the High Contracting Parties can denounce it at any time, after one year's warning, to take effect on the 31st of December of each year.

U.N. Civilian and Military
Representatives in the Congo, 1960-64

Officers in Charge[1]

1. Ralph J. Bunche (U.S.), 13 July 1960–27 August 1960
2. Andrew W. Cordier (U.S.), 27 August 1960–6 September 1960
3. Rajeshwar Dayal (India), 6 September 1960–20 May 1961
4. Indarjit Rikhye (acting) (India), 3 November 1960–
   23 November 1960
5. Mekki Abbas (acting) (Sudan), 10 March 1961– 20 May 1961
6. Sture Linner (Sweden), 20 May 1961–10 February 1962
7. Robert Gardiner (Ghana), 10 February 1962–1 May 1963
8. Max H. Dorsinville (Haiti), 1 May 1963–30 April 1964
9. Bibiano F. Osorio-Tafall (acting) (Mexico), 30 April 1964–
   30 June 1964

Representatives in Elisabethville

1. Ian E. Berendsen (New Zealand), August 1960–March 1961
2. Georges Dumontet (France), March 1961–May 1961
3. Conor Cruise O'Brien (Ireland), June 1961–November 1961
4. Brian E. Urquhart (U.K.), November 1961–January 1962
5. George Ivan Smith (acting) (Australia), December 1961
6. George Dumontet (acting) (France), 27 December 1961–
   January 1962
7. Jose Rolz-Bennett (Guatemala), January 1962–June 1962
8. Jean Back (France), June 1962
9. Eliud Mathu (Kenya), June 1962–May 1963
10. George L. Sherry (acting) (U.S.), January 1963–
11. A. Nashashibi (Jordan), May 1963–June 1964
    February 1963

[1] Until May 25, 1961, this title was *Special Representative of the Secretary-General.*

Force Commanders

1. Maj. Gen. Carl von Horn (Sweden), August 1960–December 1960
2. Lt. Gen. Sean McKeown (Ireland), January 1961–March 1962
3. Lt. Gen. Kebede Gebre (Ethiopia), April 1962–July 1963
4. Maj. Gen. Christian R. Kaldager (Norway), August 1963–December 1963
5. Maj. Gen. J. T. U. Aguiyu Ironsi (Nigeria), January 1964–June 1964

Katanga Commanders

1. Brigadier K. A. S. Raja (India), March 1961–April 1962
2. Maj. Gen. D. Prem Chand (India), May 1962–April 1963
3. Col. Worku Metaferia (acting) (Ethiopia), April 1963–June 1963
4. Brig. Gen. Abebe Teferra (Ethiopia), June 1963–June 1964

Selected Bibliography

As of early 1965 there was virtually no published research on the four-year U.N. peacekeeping operation in the Congo. The present study relies almost entirely on primary sources, including U.N. documents, official U.S. statements and reports, interviews with over a hundred persons in fifteen countries, and newspapers.

The two most useful published sources are the U.N. reports and the documentary yearbooks prepared by the Centre de Recherche et d'Information Socio-Politiques (CRISP) in Brussels. The Annual Reports of the Secretary-General of the United Nations and the Official Records of the U.N. Security Council and the U.N. General Assembly contain the U.N. record. Many important U.N. documents on the Congo are also carried in the *United Nations Review*.

The following selected titles deal with facets of the problem:

Bloomfield, Lincoln P., ed., *International Military Forces*. Boston: Little, Brown and Co., 1964. This symposium includes essays dealing with the Congo by Brian E. Urquhart, Herbert Nicholas, Stanley Hoffman, Edward H. Bowman, and James E. Fanning.

Boyd, Andrew, *United Nations: Piety, Myth, and Truth*. Harmondsworth, Middx., United Kingdom: Penguin Special S214, 1962. Chapter 6, "Flashpoint in Katanga," examines Rounds One and Two.

Burns, Arthur Lee, and Nina Heathcote, *Peace-Keeping by U.N. Forces: From Suez to the Congo*. New York: Praeger, 1963. A legal and political analysis focusing mainly on the Congo and carrying the story through February 1963.

Claude, Inis L., Jr., "United Nations Use of Military Force," *The Journal of Conflict Resolution*, Vol. VII (June 1963), pp. 117-29. An appraisal of the limits of the use of military force by the U.N.

Frank, Thomas M., and John Carey, "The Legal Aspects of the United Nations Action in the Congo." Working Paper for the Second Hammarskjold Forum, Association of the Bar of the City of New York, April 1962. Published in the Forum *Proceedings* (Lyman M. Tondel, editor), 1963. Covers the Congo operation until September 1962.

Gordon, King, *The U.N. in the Congo: A Quest for Peace*. New York: Carnegie Endowment for International Peace, 1962. An interpretative account of the operation to August 1962 by the chief information officer of the U.N. in the Congo.

Hempstone, Smith, *Rebels, Mercenaries and Dividends: The Katanga Story*. New York: Praeger, 1962. A journalistic account of the early period.

Hoffman, Stanley, "In Search of a Thread: The U.N. in the Congo Labyrinth," *International Organization*, Vol. XVI (Spring 1962), pp. 331-61.

Jacobson, Harold K., "ONUC's Civilian Operations: State-Preserving and State-Building," *World Politics*, Vol. XVII (October 1964). A summary and analysis of the UN civilian activities in the Congo in their political context. Makes a useful distinction between "state-building" and "state-preserving" on the one hand, and "nation-building" on the other.

Legum, Colin, *Congo Disaster*. Harmondsworth, Middx., United Kingdom: Penguin Special S191, 1961. A journalist's account of the first six months of independence.

Miller, E. M. (pseud.), "Legal Aspects of the United Nations Action in the Congo," *American Journal of International Law*, Vol. 55 (January 1961), pp. 1-28.

O'Brien, Conor Cruise, *To Katanga and Back*. New York: Simon and Schuster, 1962. A detailed account of O'Brien's seven-month (May-Dec., 1961) tour of duty as the U.N. representative in Elisabethville.

Rikhye, I. J., *Preparation and Training of United Nations Peacekeeping Forces*. London: Institute for Strategic Studies, Adelphi Paper No. 9, 1964. Maj. Gen. Rikhye, the military adviser to the Secretary-General, bases his comments primarily on the Congo experience. This paper was prepared for delivery at a private conference on U.N. Security Forces held in Oslo, February 1964.

Russell, Ruth B., *United Nations Experience with Military Forces: Political and Legal Aspects*. Washington: Brookings Institution Staff Paper, 1964. Forty pages of this comprehensive analysis and interpretation are devoted to the Congo effort.

Schachter, Oscar, "Preventing the Internationalization of Internal Conflict: A Legal Analysis of the U.N. Congo Experience," *Proceedings*, American Society of International Law, 1963, pp. 216-24. An authoritative interpretation by the director of the U.N. General Legal Division.

Thant, U, "A United Nations Stand-By Peace Force." Address at Cambridge, Mass., June 13, 1963. (U.N. Press Release, SG/1520, June 12, 1963.) This statement by the Secretary-General is based upon the Congo effort and other U.N. peacekeeping operations.

United Nations, *The United Nations and the Congo: Some Salient Facts*.

New York: United Nations, February 1963. This is an official U.N. "white book" on the Congo operation.

U.S. Department of State, *U.S. Participation in the U.N.* Annual reports by the President to the Congress, for the years 1960, 1961, 1962, 1963, and 1964. Washington, D.C.: Government Printing Office.

Watkins, Tarleton H., "The Congo Airlift," *Air University Quarterly Review*, Vol. 13, No. 1 (Summer 1961), pp. 19-33. Brig. Gen. Watkins discusses the U.S. airlift for the first three months of the operation.

Wigny, Pierre, "Belgium and the Congo," *International Affairs*, Vol. 37 (July 1961), pp. 273-84. An official Belgian interpretation of events immediately before and after independence by the Minister of Foreign Affairs, 1958-61.

Index